Vanilla or Chocolate,
Nuts or Not,
Cone or Cup . . .
Young or old . . .
When you get to have
Ice cream it takes ya
back to your happiest
memories.

Guy Fieri

I love foo♡ W9-BUS-990
food!!! I am happy to see
people take a creative approach
to ice cream while embracing
their sexuality and incorporating
the two into an AWESOME
creation of wonder.

James Deen

Hey D&B,
Thanks for all
that milk Money.
Sorry I called
you gay.

Jim Gaffigan

READ this BOOK!!!
Doug & Bryan MAKE MY DAMN
MötleyCRüE look like A Buncha
Singing nuns.-.

Tommy Lee

Dear Bryan and Doug
Thank goodness for
your sweet sauces
and toppings. They've
gotten me through
some tough times
and make my day
tastier!

♡ Alex
Alex Guarnaschelli

DAMN BiG GAY
ice Yum bang pimpmycone
unicorn mofos rock my hungry
happy tongue.....chillified fantastico!!
Wheeeee-

Mario Batali

Oct. 19, 1987

This is to inform the student body that Douglas Quint has been suspended from the Bassoon Ensemble, effective immediately. He shall also no longer be welcome at band practice, Glee Club, school athletic events, or public gatherings of any kind while in possession of his instrument. It is the feeling of the faculty that his presence has proven, again and again, to be disruptive. The bassoon, as we have stressed to young Mr. Quint many times, is a powerful tool and its strange and terrible powers (not unlike nuclear energy) are to be used for Good--not Evil.

Sadly, I must also announce the expulsion of another student, Bryan Petroff, for the unauthorized sale of what are apparently homemade ice cream and dairy products from the trunk of his car during school hours. As has been explained to Bryan, there are rules governing the sale and distribution of foodstuffs--and from all evidence available, his "business" is in violation of nearly all of them.

Clearly the widespread abuse of sugary frozen treats with ironic names like "The Bea Arthur" and "The Salty [procurer]" is not in the best interests of an institution of learning and its student body--no matter how delicious or whimsical. While I am myself a longtime admirer of the oeuvre of fashion icon Ms. Bea Arthur, particularly her work on the classic television series _Maude_, I doubt very much whether she would want herself remembered as a soft-serve ice cream cone sold out of the trunk of a battered El Camino with a unicorn mural on its doors.

Speaking of said vehicle:

Mr. Frebesher, of the English Department, points out that the term "Big Gay Ice Cream Truck," the name emblazoned rather gaudily on its hood under a frolicking unicorn, is perhaps a misnomer. Is the El Camino actually a "truck," per se? Or is it more of a half-truck/half-coupe? Also, when we say "big gay ice cream truck," is it the ice cream or the truck itself to which we are attributing "gay" qualities? Are Messrs. Quint and Petroff implying that there is something "gay" about eating ice cream--a delicious summer treat, which all of us, heterosexual or not, enjoy regardless of our personal lifestyle choices? The wording is ambiguous.

In other campus news, the Fighting Unicorns face off against the Springfield Ferrets on Chiswick Field this Friday night. Due to popular demand, Beef Noodle Casserole has been added to the menu, Chicken Hawaiian having been removed.

A reminder--and there are no exceptions--that jackets and ties are still required on Wednesdays for assembly and that gentlemen's hair must still reach no further than collar or earlobe. Hiding your actual locks under a Dynel pixie-cut wig is not an acceptable option.

Skirting, evading, or violating the rules is no way to get ahead.

As a postscript, let me suggest that any students approached by either Mr. Quint or Mr. Petroff with an offer to contribute to their purported "book" resist the urge and immediately report the incident to me.

This project is clearly doomed.

Veritas Fortissima!

Monsignor Anthony Bourdain
Headmaster

BIG GAY
ICE CREAM

Saucy Stories & Frozen Treats:
Going All the Way with Ice Cream

Bryan Petroff and Douglas Quint
with Rebecca Flint Marx

Photographs by Donny Tsang • Illustrations by Jason O'Malley

Clarkson Potter/Publishers
New York

Published in the United States by Clarkson Potter/Publishers,
an imprint of the Crown Publishing Group, a division of Random
House LLC, a Penguin Random House Company, New York.

www.crownpublishing.com
www.clarksonpotter.com

CLARKSON POTTER is a trademark and POTTER with colophon
is a registered trademark of Random House LLC.

Big Gay Ice Cream, Big Gay Ice Cream Truck, Monday Sundae,
Salty Pimp, Choinkwich, American Globs, Gobbler, Mermaid,
cone logo, mud logo, and unicorn logo are all trademarks of
Big Gay Inc.

Recipe on page 124, "Chocolate Cookies," from the *Treats
Truck Baking Book* by Kim Ima. Copyright © 2011 by Kim Ima.
Reprinted by permission of HarperCollins Publishers.

Recipe on page 144, "Cheater Soft-Serve Ice Cream," from
The Truck Food Cookbook. Copyright © 2012 by John T. Edge.
Used by permission of Workman Publishing Co., Inc, New York.
All rights reserved.

Library of Congress Cataloging-in-Publication Data
Petroff, Bryan.
Big gay ice cream / Bryan Petroff and Douglas Quint;
with Rebecca Marx Flint ; foreword by Anthony Bourdain ;
photographs by Donny Tsang.—First edition.
pages cm
Includes index.
1. Ice cream, ices, etc. I. Quint, Douglas. II. Title.
TX795.P486 2015
641.86'2—dc23
2014022856

ISBN 978-0-385-34560-6
eBook ISBN 978-0-385-34561-3

Printed in China

Book design and illustrations by Jason O'Malley
Cover design by Jess Morphew
Photographs by Donny Tsang

10 9 8 7 6 5 4 3 2 1

First Edition

For our mothers, Mary and Patricia.

Clearly they deserve most of the blame
(our therapists want us to change that to "credit")
for this whole saga.

For our Big Gay Godmother, Mindy Novack,
who fought for us every step of the way.

Contents

SPECIAL
memories
I'll never forget that.
time under the ~~bleachers~~
Bleachers! Stay true,
Andy Rich

Freshman
Year

ICE CREAM 101

ORIENTATION
Honey, I bought a big gay ice cream truck!

In the Beginning . . .

We never decided to have a business together—it just happened. In 2009, we were sitting at home. Like any modern couple, we were farting around on our laptops on opposite ends of the sofa, when Doug noticed that his friend Andrea Fisher had posted on Facebook, looking for ice cream truck drivers.

Doug and Andrea had met at Juilliard, where he was studying the bassoon and she the flute. Doug had always been jealous of Andrea because she had the balls to do stuff like spend her summers in Japan, where she earned cash as a stripper. The last time Doug was in Japan, he visited a coed pool with a therapeutic electrical current running through it. Although it was clothing optional, his local translator informed him he'd need to keep a washcloth over his naughty bits because, well, he might scare the locals. Dreams of a nudity-based Asian income stream came crumbling down.

Andrea had been driving an ice cream truck for a few years, and the New York Times had written a story about her. So when Doug saw Andrea's post, he decided to sign up. As a concert bassoonist working on his doctorate at The CUNY Graduate Center, he spent winters commuting to Boston to play and summers in New York making reeds and praying for work. He was tired of commuting and thought it would

be fun to make money instead of living on ramen. Also, he wanted to spend more time with Bryan. We had only moved in together about six months prior. Our first date (and first time meeting face-to-face) was at a Barnes & Noble to hear Charlotte Rae, Mrs. Garrett on The Facts of Life, sing songs from an album (Songs I Taught My Mother) that she had recorded decades earlier and was seeing a new release. Olympia Dukakis was also there ("Would you call this cullah grape or aubergine?"), and we took that as a good sign. Sign of what, exactly, we didn't know.

No Experience Required

Neither one of us had ever worked in the food business before, much less driven a Mister Softee truck, so we decided to start a blog about it. We had no idea how the whole thing was going to work. We didn't know how to get licenses, permits, or anything, and we thought it would be fun (if not for our friends, then certainly for us) to document our adventures.

Before Doug announced our presence online, though, we needed a name for our truck. Originally "Big Gay Ice Cream Truck" was just a placeholder, but people started following us on social media because they got a kick out of seeing "I'm a fan of the Big Gay Ice Cream Truck" in their feed. Most people thought it was an elaborate joke, and honestly, all these years later, in its own surreal way, it still is. We reached out to our friend Jason (an ex of Bryan), who came up with our cone logo, and the silly name and imagery created a fan base months before our launch.

Doug was missing a few of the essentials when the truck's owner gave Andrea the green light to find additional drivers for his fleet—namely, blond hair and big tits. The owner laughed out loud when we showed him our logo and told him, "We really just want to rent the truck and do our own thing." But he gave us the go-ahead, and then the work began, including sales tax certification, mobile food vendor licenses for each of us, and miscellaneous Department of Health (DOH) shit, along with creating the menu, sourcing ingredients, and taste-testing.

Bryan suggested doing unusual toppings as a way of modernizing the ice cream truck experience. It was 2009 and time to move beyond the decades-long tradition of Mister Softee dips and sprinkles.

This was a chance to escape from reality a bit, to ditch Bryan's corporate life and leave Doug's grad school behind and just have fun, be creative, and basically do whatever the hell we wanted, without any worries about how it would turn out. We honestly didn't know what to expect or how long it would last—four days? Four weeks? Four hours?! But we wanted to make sure it would be a blast for us, whether it took off like wildfire or crashed in a blaze of (non)glory.

The Big Gay Menu

Bryan's menu inspiration got its initial spark 2,906 miles from the nearest NYC Mister Softee truck: Pizzeria Picco, in Larkspur, California (north of San Francisco). They had a soft-serve machine and offered only vanilla ice cream but spruced it up with toppings.

We started holding taste-testing parties for our friends with all of our topping ideas, using store-bought ice cream like Edy's and Breyer's, whipped a bit like we did when we were young to mimic soft-serve. We'd do things like try eight different kinds of olive oil and then vote for our favorite. A lot of inspiration came from walking into grocery stores and seeing what was on the shelves. We knew what flavors we liked, and we also knew what we didn't want to be: TCBY or Tasti D-Lite or Pinkberry or 16 Handles or blahblahblah. That meant things like M&M's, Gummi Bears, and breakfast cereal were verboten.

The first toppings we offered on the truck were olive oil and sea salt, Trix (we broke our "no breakfast cereal" rule because Trix is so intrinsically queer), dulce de leche, ginger syrup, curry powder, Nilla wafers, spices like cayenne and cardamom, and fresh berries tossed in saba—a thick grape reduction that we were introduced to by a great Italian restaurant, Franny's, in Brooklyn. We also made floats with high-quality small-batch sodas. By the middle of that first summer in 2009, we'd started making creative sundaes, and by our second season, we'd come up with fun names for them.

INVU4URAQT!
xo Jack

CLASS SLUT

Before Doug got into ice cream, I had been doing it for three summers. I started driving an ice cream truck on a drunken dare when a friend and I passed by the Kool Man depot in Williamsburg, Brooklyn. It was 2006, I had just graduated from Juilliard, and I needed a job.

After working the mean streets of Bed-Stuy and East New York, getting my tires slashed numerous times, being punched by a customer, and finding a gun held up in front of my truck at a block party, I quit "the business." But I found myself needing a job again, and so I visited another depot in Greenpoint, Brooklyn, owned by a competitor (a guy I always fought with at McCarren Park-- he admitted to having his friend slash my tires). Long story short, we became cool. I worked for him in Manhattan for the summer, and his team loved me, so he wanted me to recruit more drivers, "hot girls" like me, for the next season. I got a cut from each driver I brought on.

My Facebook ad was just to see if any of my girlfriends were interested, but I knew Doug from Juilliard, when I'd been a flute student there. His job as orchestral manager was to kick my ass for showing up high at early morning rehearsals, but we became friends outside Juilliard.

"I'm totally interested in working for you," he told me. "How much is the vendor badge? I wouldn't have to beat up any competitors, right? The spots are places that wouldn't cause a hassle? Lemme know. If the badge isn't a billion dollars, I'll get it, and if I don't end up with some AMAZING GIG next summer (bwahahahahahah), I'll do whatever you want."

Why not? He's not a hot girl, but he's gay, so that could work. I guided him (and then Bryan) through the vending badge/tax-ID process from hell, and suddenly Doug was getting press before he even started working! Soon, Doug was everyone's favorite worker (besides me, of course) at the depot.

Andrea Fisher

That's our BGIC Trucker, Genevieve

Doug had a beef with the typically surly ice cream truck operators who'd take your order while yakking away on their Bluetooth headsets. Why would you want to give your money to someone who's talking to someone else on their phone?! He wanted to be really nice to people—which he ultimately found to be exhausting but gratifying. We were the Big Gay Ice Cream Truck, after all! Every customer had to walk away having had a fun and kooky experience.

We're Off!

We intended to start serving on the streets a few weeks before our very first event, Brooklyn Gay Pride. Getting the city to grant a mobile vending license is not simply a long, tedious process, it's an ordeal—and our vendor badges didn't arrive until the day before Brooklyn Pride. We didn't even get on the truck until the day of the event, but somehow it worked out. We had fun, although we didn't know what we were doing. Kim Severson from the *New York Times* was there, acting as sort of den mother, Doubting Thomas, and cheerleader. Andrea was there, too, scamming people on prices. That Andrea!

A week later, we were out on the streets, parked at what would become "our corner," Broadway and 17th Street, at Union Square. That first summer we were in our own strange world, soaking up how crazy and fun the whole idea was. We had all sorts coming to the truck: kids, the occasional celebrity, fashionistas, gym rats, incognito food writers, junkies, and uninitiated people who stood in line thinking we were a normal truck until they got to the window and saw all of these weird toppings and our Big Gay Sign.

That first summer saw the convergence of food trucks and social media, and we were extremely fortunate to have been there. People were really getting into social media, and its growing popularity mirrored and influenced ours. What started out as simple tweets about our locations and specials quickly turned into Doug's outlet for irreverent humor and insight and became our platform to build our brand. The first few hundred people who followed us on Twitter that summer were outrageously helpful and loyal. If Doug tweeted that he was thirsty, someone would show up a minute or two later with sodas. And our Twitter following continued to grow by the thousands over the dead of winter, when the truck wasn't even out—we were on to something. Twitter was where Doug asked for a name for one of our most popular cones, which consisted of vanilla ice cream with smashed-up Nilla wafers and some dulce de leche. Someone suggested The Golden Girl because of the color. Bea Arthur had just passed away, so we named the cone after her. The Choinkwich, our bacon-chocolate ice cream sandwich, was also a product of Twitter.

The summer of 2009 concluded at the Vendy Awards, an annual event that celebrates street-food vendors. We were the first (and only, as of this writing) truck to be nominated in two categories in the same year. Unfortunately, we didn't win either award, but we still ended the season on a high note, having achieved our goals to have fun and at least break even.

During the winter, Doug went back to playing bassoon and Bryan continued working full-time in human resources at a fashion company. By our third year, though, we'd realized

HALL MONITOR

The boys were so cute that muddy Sunday at the Brooklyn gay pride festival. There they were, acting like they knew what they were doing, their banged-up Mr. Softee truck rigged with a sign trumpeting their bigness and their gayness.

I paid three dollars for a cone for my toddler. "That's a lot of money for street ice cream, no matter how gay or proud you are," I thought. "They'll never last." Still, I admired their efforts. Was that saba they were drizzling over my swirl? A year later, my daughter was demanding a cone and sprinkles, and I saw the boys' tweet. They were in the 'hood! Sprinkles for her, a cone with fig sauce, olive oil, and sea salt for me. They told me they were going to be on The Rachael Ray Show. Smell you, Nancy Drew!

In the months that followed, they kept showing up in the Twitter feeds of the rich and famous. Pictures of fancy New York celebrities eating gay ice cream populated my inbox. The next thing I knew, they were opening a real store. Apparently their little hobby was going to pay off. As we say in the Deep South, where I currently reside, you boys are living in the high cotton now.

Kim Severson

that Big Gay Ice Cream was our life. We opened a Big Gay Ice Cream Shop in the East Village over Labor Day weekend 2011: a contrabassoon octet serenaded the neighbors, drag queens and roller derby girls roamed the street, and Anthony Bourdain, dressed as a priest, offered his benediction: "May you go forward and make a shitload of money! Sell a lot of motherfuckin' ice cream!" And we did. We had lines down the block. A year later, we opened in the West Village, our second shop, easy to find with its giant unicorn on the window.

Which Brings Us to the Book

We've been on a pretty wild ride. It's been hectic and challenging, overwhelming and gratifying, but never boring. This book may be as unconventional as our story. And just as we've always wanted to provide our customers with a friendly, accessible (though perhaps bizarre) experience, we wanted to give you equally fun and friendly ice cream recipes.

Welcome to our yearbook, which follows our evolution from trembling freshmen to lofty seniors. Our recipes follow a similar trajectory. You'll find the most basic ones at the beginning: store-bought topping ideas and simple combinations that lead to recipes for homemade toppings and sauces. As juniors, you'll learn how to create concoctions like shakes, floats, sundaes, and the infamous Choinkwich. Finally, as seniors, you'll find actual ice cream recipes. These recipes start with relatively simple sorbets and no-cook eggless ice creams, then move up to egg-based ice creams.

For far too many people, homemade ice cream is a frightening concept. One that conjures up images of expensive machines, scrambled eggs, and moderate-to-intense heartbreak. We're here to tell—and show—you that it doesn't have to be any of those things. On the contrary, all you need to make ice cream at home is a sense of adventure (and lactose tolerance). A child-like sense of wonder also helps, because really, is there any food that more perfectly summons our inner child? We firmly believe, and our customers surely agree, that ice cream is meant to be a fun food, and so making it should be fun, too.

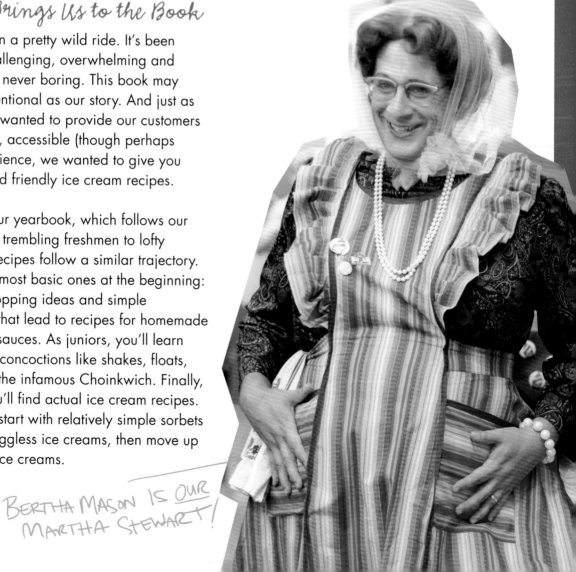

BERTHA MASON IS OUR MARTHA STEWART!

With our guidance, you can expand your own frozen treat repertoire—and, most important, have fun doing it! Besides, if that ice cream maker is only going to sit in your freezer collecting ice crystals, you may as well get it out of there and use the freezer space for more important things, like vodka.

Having fun with ice cream doesn't mean you have to bone up on your egg-tempering skills and make it yourself. There are plenty of ways to spruce up store-bought ice cream. In fact, we think it's a smart idea to just keep vanilla ice cream in your home freezer and then create your own endless array of combinations and flavors from your pantry and fridge.

So, let's start with this scenario: It's Friday night. A gaggle of Beckys are on their way over. You're going to watch a Ryan Gosling movie marathon, paint each other's toenails, and compare boyfriends. You don't have time to make your favorite dinner (ice cream) from scratch, because you have more important things to do (blend up pitchers of margaritas). But you do have a half gallon of vanilla in your freezer. What do you do?

Well, you did get an A in Home Ec, didn't you? I mean, who didn't? So put on your "thinking apron," open those pantry doors, and get creative.

THAT'S ROY CHOI, THE GODFATHER OF STREETFOOD

STOCKING YOUR PANTRY & FRIDGE

Shopping The Supermarket

You don't have to go to specialty shops to find tasty options for your ice cream. You can find plenty at your standard large-scale supermarket, but go to every section *except* the ice cream toppings aisle. Instead, look for the following:

- **FRESH FRUIT, FRESH VEGETABLES,** and **FRESH HERBS**

- **INTERNATIONAL** and **KOSHER FOODS:** tamari, halva, hot sauces, matcha, Thai iced tea mix, etc.

- **COOKIES, CEREALS, GRANOLAS,** and **POP TARTS**

- **JAMS, JELLIES, MARMALADES, NUTS,** and **NUT BUTTERS**

- **BREAKFAST SYRUPS:** maple, but also fun stuff like blueberry syrup

- **OLIVE OILS:** something very green and supervirginal

- **VINEGARS:** plain, flavored, or infused

- **SALTS, PEPPERS, CHILIES, SPICES,** and **DRIED HERBS**

- **CANDY:** be creative—avoid Gummi Bears, and go with espresso malt balls!

TOOLS & EQUIPMENT

Here is a list of equipment we recommend keeping in your kitchen. As our good friends the Girl Scouts always say, "We're more prepared than the Boy Scouts."

Basic Stuff

- **SQUEEZE BOTTLES** for drizzling sauces. You can cut off the tips to make apertures of varying sizes.

- **1-QUART PLASTIC CONTAINERS** (aka plastic Chinese takeout soup containers) for storing sauces, toppings, and your homemade ice creams

- **FUNNELS** for transferring sauces to squeeze bottles

- **MICROPLANES** for grating zest, spices, etc.

- **ICE CREAM SCOOPS** (or else you'll mangle lots of spoons, trust us)

- **SPREADERS** (easier than knives for lining cones and making ice cream sandwiches)

A Little More Advanced

- **COFFEE/SPICE GRINDER** (toast and grind your own whole spices instead of buying spice powders)

- **DOUBLE BOILER** (will save you from ruining batches of chocolate sauce and other items prone to burning)

- **GOOD SHARP KNIVES** (and knife guards)

- **SALT & PEPPER MILLS**

- **CANDY THERMOMETER**

- **SILICONE SPATULAS** (never use rubber ones when cooking hot foods)

- **DIGITAL KITCHEN SCALE**

- **FRENCH PRESS**

- **FINE-MESH CONICAL STRAINER** (China cap)

Serious Gear

- **IMMERSION BLENDER** for pureeing sauces

- **JUICER** (the freshest juice really does make the best sorbet)

- **ICE CREAM MACHINE** (see page 136 for our recommendations)

- **WHIPPED CREAM DISPENSER** and chargers

SIMPLE TOPPING IDEAS

Here are some really tasty topping ideas specifically geared for the ice cream Triple Crown of vanilla, chocolate, and strawberry.

SPECIAL
FUN TOPPINGS!
+ $1.00

SPECIAL
PEPPERMINT SYRUP
+ cocoa nibs
(scharfenberger)

SPECIAL
WASABI
pea dust

SPECIAL
OLIVE OIL
+ sea salt
(Bariani, Northern Cal.)

SPECIAL
TRIX
cereal

t Ice Cream

VANILLA

HONEY & CAYENNE

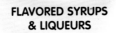

FLAVORED SYRUPS
& LIQUEURS

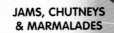

MAPLE SYRUP

JAMS, CHUTNEYS
& MARMALADES

CACAO NIBS

CARDAMOM

FRUIT BUTTERS

PEANUT BRITTLE

BALSAMIC
VINEGAR

OLIVE OIL

TRIX

CARAMEL

CHOCOLATE

COCOA PUFFS

HOT SAUCE

PEPPERMINT CANDIES

GINGER SYRUP & CURRY POWDER

SHARP CHEDDAR CHEESE & FRESH CHERRIES

MALT BALLS

CANDIED FENNEL SEEDS

COCONUT

See you in morning bowl next year old
xo

PISTACHIOS

CHILIES

GRAND
MARNIER

SALT

ORANGE
MARMALADE

OLD BAY
SEASONING

CHOCOLATE-COVERED
ESPRESSO BEANS

CARAMEL &
SEA SALT

STRAWBERRY

SHORTBREAD
COOKIES

BASIL

MACADAMIA NUTS

SABA

JALAPEÑO

ELDERFLOWER
SYRUP

MINI
MARSHMALLOWS

PEANUT BUTTER

WHITE CHOCOLATE

PEPPERCORNS

PINEAPPLE & MINT

TARRAGON

LEMONGRASS

INFUSED & FLAVORED BALSAMIC VINEGARS

Show choir will be so meh ☺ without you guys!
xo

VANILLA

HONEY For added kick, stir in a pinch of cayenne or a few drops of chili oil and then drizzle over.

OLIVE OIL High-quality olive oil and sea salt give vanilla a deep, buttery taste.

CACAO NIBS (crushed, roasted cocoa beans that have been separated from their husks) Sprinkle some over and drizzle with peppermint syrup for the ultimate Peppermint Pattie.

FLAVORED SYRUPS & LIQUEURS Look for high-quality flavored coffee syrups and liqueurs. A favorite is Ginger People brand ginger syrup, with or without a dusting of mild yellow curry powder.

TRIX We usually avoid cereal as a topping, since every yogurt and ice cream shop in the country does it, but we break our own rule for two: Trix and Cocoa Puffs. Both look amazing on vanilla (think kids' party) and taste great.

BALSAMIC VINEGAR In addition to straight-up balsamic, look for flavored balsamics: apple, fig, blood orange. These all marry well with olive oil and sea salt.

MAPLE SYRUP Go with richer, darker Grade B syrup.

FRUIT BUTTERS Blueberry, peach, apple, pumpkin— all great for a pie à la mode sundae.

CARDAMOM Lightly sprinkle on some cardamom powder. Delish!

CARAMEL Spoon some of this over, then add a generous sprinkling of sea salt.

JAMS, CHUTNEYS & MARMALADES A big spoonful of any of these.

CHOCOLATE

CHILIES Add some heat to your ice cream. Try cayenne pepper and chipotle chili powder.

SALT Sprinkle on some Maldon regular or smoked sea salt.

PISTACHIOS Particularly spicy ones, like red-chili-roasted pistachios.

SALTED NUTS (VARIOUS) Salted Spanish peanuts on chocolate were a favorite of Doug's father. Crushed macadamias are a favorite of Bryan's.

CARAMELIZED BACON 'Nuff said.

HOT SAUCE We especially love Sriracha.

GINGER SYRUP & CURRY POWDER While good over vanilla, this combination is great over chocolate.

COCONUT Toasted coconut flakes are great.

CARAMEL With some sea salt sprinkled over to spike the flavors.

CANDIED FENNEL SEEDS Look for these at Indian groceries or order online.

COCOA PUFFS For a double-chocolate punch.

OLD BAY SEASONING There is no food that Old Bay isn't awesome on—ice cream included. It adds so much depth. You need to try this.

ORANGE MARMALADE A big spoonful.

SHARP CHEDDAR CHEESE & FRESH CHERRIES Fact: The act of grating cheddar cheese over chocolate ice cream makes you eligible to vote in Wisconsin!

GRAND MARNIER For anyone who loves chocolate paired with fruit, you'll appreciate what Grand Marnier's orange flavor brings to your ice cream. Plus, it's booze.

STRAWBERRY

SABA Ready to go beyond balsamic? Try this rich, syrupy grape reduction.

PINEAPPLE Use small cubes. Also great combined with a chiffonade of fresh mint.

JALAPEÑO Sprinkle on some finely diced fresh or candied jalapeño pepper.

BASIL A chiffonade of basil, which is actually a member of the mint family, is fantastic.

ELDERFLOWER Use the syrup or St-Germain liqueur.

CRUSHED MACADAMIA NUTS Macadamias have a meaty quality, and we love adding a crunchy element to any ice cream.

INFUSED & FLAVORED VINEGARS Look for flavored balsamics: apple, fig, blood orange.

LEMONGRASS Use the extract or the jarred finely sliced variety from your supermarket's always-peculiar Asian Foods aisle.

WHITE CHOCOLATE Use a vegetable peeler to shower some shavings over the top.

PEANUT BUTTER Think PB&J.

PEPPERCORNS Crack over some pink or Sichuan peppercorns.

SHORTBREAD COOKIES Break up and sprinkle.

MINI MARSHMALLOWS Try brûléeing the marshmallows.

FRESH FRUIT Mix and match your favorite in-season fruit.

TARRAGON A sprinkle of this creates a wormhole from your kitchen to Provence.

ROBITUSSIN (We kid! Don't try it!)

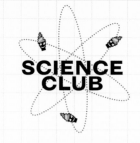

SCIENCE CLUB

Why Does Salt Make Ice Colder?

Water normally freezes at 0°C (32°F). Saltwater freezes at about −21°C (around −6°F), so it stays in liquid form at lower temperatures than plain water. The addition of salt means ice that was solid, at, say, 25°F, will become a liquid at that same temperature. You see how salting icy roads in winter makes sense, right?

With an old-fashioned ice cream maker, the ice you put into it will melt at the normal ice/liquid transition temperature, 32°F. At this temperature, the ice is melting and refreezing at the same rate. But when you add salt, the ice that melts won't refreeze until the temperature gets a lot lower. So, as the ice/liquid temperature gets lower, it will draw heat from anywhere it can—namely, your soon-to-be ice cream.

If you think that's cool, skip the sodium chloride (regular salt) and go to your local hardware store for some calcium chloride. It will lower the freezing point even more, down to −29°C (−20°F). That would ice your cream a lot faster!

LINING CONES

Think of the inside of cones as unused real estate. If an ice cream cone gets a topping, we tell our staff that a little of the topping also goes down into the empty cone. Some customers want an extra wallop of flavor and ask for their cones fully lined. There's pretty much an endless mix-and-match game you can play with these tasty schmears.

- Nut butters

- Chocolate-hazelnut spread (e.g., Nutella)

- Speculoos spread (e.g., Biscoff)

- Dulce de leche or caramel sauce

- Chocolate sauce or spread

- Any sauce from our Sophomore section (see pages 53–73)

- Jams, preserves, or marmalades

- Vegemite

- Balsamic vinegar

- Olive oil and a bit of sea salt

- Fruit curds or butters

Best Friends Forever! Stay cool this summer. And NOW you know why they call me 'Donut Tits'. —Caroline Pierce

Ice Cream Social Playlist

N.R. ☐YES ☐NO

60

UR
POSITION
NORMAL
TYPE I

UR
POSITION
IEC TYPE I • NORMAL

maxell

SHARK WEEK!

A DATE ___ N.R.
☐YES ☐NO

B DATE ___ N.R.
☐YES ☐NO

Romeo Void
"Never Say Never"

Hanson
"MMMBop"

Christeene
"African Mayonnaise"

Eileen Barton
"If I Knew You Were
Comin' I'd've
Baked a Cake"

Johnny Cash
"Cocaine Blues"

Klaus Nomi
"Ding Dong the Witch
Is Dead"

The Coasters
"Riot in Cell Block #9"

David Bowie
"Scary Monsters (and
Super Creeps)"

Stargard
"Theme from Up
Which Way Is Up"

Destiny's Child
"Bootylicious"

Violent Femmes
"Gone Daddy Gone"

Prince
"Starfish and Coffee"

Annette Funicello
"Pineapple Princess"

Captain Beefheart
"Ice Cream for Crow"

Redd Kross
"Super Sunny Christmas"

DJ Cutlet
"Big Gay Ice Cream Truck"

Jane Wiedlin
"Big Gay Ice Cream Song"

Sophomore Year

DRESS UP YOUR ICE CREAM WITH HOMEMADE TOPPINGS AND SAUCES

CHOKING!

Ask "ARE YOU CHOKING?"
Call 911 if person can't speak or breathe.

IF PERSON IS AWAKE:

Make a fist.

Place it above the person's belly button, well below the rib cage.

Pull sharply, inward and upward.

Continue until the food comes out or the person can breathe.

IF PERSON STOPS RESPONDING:

Open the mouth. If food is there, take it out. If food is not visible, tilt the person's head back.

Pinch the person's nose. Place your mouth over the person's mouth and give two breaths.

Push hard repeatedly in chest center for 20 seconds. Check breathing. Repeat from start.

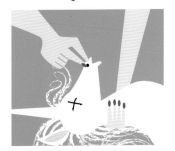

HEALTH CLASS
The Wonderful World Of NYC Food Vendor Certification

What the Hell Is Mental Hygiene?

Anyone serving food on the streets of New York needs to have two things: (1) a New York State sales tax authorization number, issued by the Department of Consumer Affairs, and (2) a valid New York City Mobile Food Vendor License from the Department of Health and Mental Hygiene. It doesn't matter if you want to fry a lamb, boil a peanut, swirl a cone, or simply hand an apple to a customer, or whether you are self-employed or an employee of a well-established company, a hired driver, or the owner of a food truck. Every person selling food on the street must be licensed by both the state and city. Obtaining these permits requires the same two things that any form of government-issued documentation will cost you: your sanity and your time. Years later, we still don't even know what the phrase "mental hygiene" means.

At a restaurant, there only needs to be one person on-site with a Food Handler's Permit (the brick-and-mortar equivalent of the mobile license). You could be a bustling 400-seat Times Square restaurant employing over 50 people per shift, and only one person needs to be trained in proper food handling and preparation. A dishwasher (with no authority or supervision over others) will suffice as a permit holder. And, unlike the truck's requirement of individual sales tax certification (on top of the mobile license), no one in a restaurant needs to possess any documentation related to sales tax—a rather blatant example of New York City's efforts to make mobile vending as cumbersome as possible.

Obtaining a vendor license (called "the badge" on the streets) required a two-day DOH course that was offered only once a month. At the time, no information about class scheduling was available via phone or website. Week after week, Doug trudged down to this wretched office purgatory; time after time, the class was scheduled for when he had to be out of town.

The class was held in a big old school in East Harlem. The school steps were commandeered by fellow DOH class pupils yelling into Bluetooth headsets in a cacophony of the many languages that make up the Big Apple.

We convened in a basement classroom with small windows near the ceiling that offered views of the ankles of passersby obscured by filthy chicken wire. The only fixture of interest in the room was a gleaming, sparkling hot dog cart that had never seen street warfare. Class began, but the chattering, arguments, and text messaging continued. Did the parents of our fellow classmates force them to attend this? As our teacher informed us, our dreams were about to come true. "Welcome to America! This is it! You are living your dream!" Was Doug's dream to safely dispense boiled hot dogs? Was Bryan's dream to use deli paper when grabbing a doughnut to avoid passing on "the bacteria"? We weren't so sure, and the city's heartfelt welcome to this country was around forty years too late.

Dread and doubt escalated with every tick of the clock. What the hell were we doing? Was this really what we had signed up for? Was listening to stories of acrylic nails ending up in people's salad bars worth leaving our paying jobs? Was hearing a laundry list of airborne illnesses broken down by fish-borne ones versus canned-food-borne ones worth it, all just to introduce homosexual dairy products to NYC?

Doug wanted a weird summer job and he was certainly getting his money's worth. Bryan, at this point in the game, was just playing dutiful spouse, along for the ride. We were Clark and Ellen Griswold. The notion of success or failure (or a mash-up of the two) fascinated Doug. Bryan had already chalked up the whole thing to a midlife crisis, but now realized it could be more of a downward shame spiral.

The textbook was fascinating, and it made Doug ponder why instructional line drawings are so underrated. If they are good enough to show us how to escape from a plane after a water landing, they are good enough to teach us the glory of the hairnet. One showed the difference between an excellent food handler (with a hairnet, gloves, and a squeaky clean, shiny glow) and an abhorrent food handler (complete with ratty hair, Band-Aids, dirt smudges, and what appeared to be track marks).

Doug supposed the teaching method employed by the class's two instructors might be labeled "call and response"—better suited for cheerleading and *Showtime at the Apollo*. The teacher posed a question, and then students shouted answers without thought or regard. The responses were more visceral than cerebral.

Teacher: "When should you wash your hands?"

Student: "After you take a shit!"

Teacher: "That's right! After a bowel movement. Good!"

For real.

We learned that "the virus" can be killed with "the bleach," and that meats needed to be refrigerated. Meanwhile, two twenty-something Greek guys tried to pick up a girl in the row ahead of them with, "Hey, baby," but she didn't buy it.

No one, including the teacher (who insisted that it was a mistake in the workbook), understood why a hot dog would be classified as a precooked food, the lone exception on the list of meats that had to be cooked to a specific temperature. The teacher said that the city has always had this wrong; it doesn't make sense to say that you are merely reheating the hot dog, because, he emphasized, a hot dog comes out of the package raw. Maybe someone should have told him the basics of meat slurry, curing, and smoking, or at least directed him to the "fully cooked" label on hot dog packages. But some things are probably best left to self-discovery.

SPECIAL $6

Hot Chocolate!
ur spicy home-brew
ver Vanilla Ice cream
th Whipped Cream.

SPECIAL

TRY THIS! $5
le FIG SAUCE
VE OIL
SALT

L $6⁰⁰
Sundae
ream

THAT'S WRITER
JORDANA ROTHMAN
AND PHOTOGRAPHER
DANIEL KRIEGER
GIVING US AN
AWARD!

E. coli versus salmonella. *Trichinella spiralis* versus *Listeria*. 145°F versus 155°F versus 165°F. There was the Food Danger Zone (between 40° and 140°F), proper storing in refrigerators (don't put dripping raw chicken over your veggies), and what song to sing while washing your hands ("Happy Birthday"—three times).

When I Become a Vendor, Will I Dream in Farsi?

The second and final class session began with an hour-long review of everything we'd learned the night before. Doug spent the time studying for the Doctoral Comprehensive Exam that he had to take the next morning at CUNY. Then came the test, offered in multiple languages: English and Spanish, naturally, but also French, Farsi, Polish, Hindi, Punjabi, Vietnamese, several Chinese dialects, and another five or so others. Doug considered taking it in a language completely foreign to him but wimped out. We both finished the fifteen-question test in roughly twenty-eight seconds.

We graduated, but there was no pomp and circumstance and our dream was still a few months away. Each student was handed a signed letter as proof that he had successfully completed the course, and we were required to take these back to the Department of Consumer Affairs and return at a later date to have pictures taken for our badges. Then we had to wait for Albany to laminate our faces and mail them back to us. All in the name of soft-serve!

But between the instructional line drawings and hand-washing intel, it wasn't a complete waste of time. And, in case you were wondering, Doug passed his doctoral comprehensive exams the next morning. Those took approximately seven hours and thirty minutes longer than the mobile vendor exam.

Why Do Something Once, When You Can Do It Twice at Double the Price?

When it came time to open our first shop, we had to go through this all over again because we needed to have a Food Handler's Permit. It was back to school for us. Instead of a three-hour class followed by a test, this time it was a fifteen-chapter online course, followed by a quiz on each chapter, followed by an in-person test.

We got a temporary permit, and then it was up to us to make sure that the water in our sinks was hot enough to scald your flesh off, up to us to throw away outdated milk, and up to us to make sure that our shop scored an "A" when the Department of Health came a callin'.

TOPPINGS

OK, kiddies, it's time to bang the pots and pans, start tossing around your knives and other pointy objects, and make your own toppings. Now we're cooking with gas.

Mixed Fruit & Saba MAKES 1 CUP

Saba may be a new ingredient for you. It's a syrup made from reduced grape must. You may say, oh, you mean balsamic? Actually, no, more like if molasses came from grapes. Saba isn't a vinegar, has no bite, and is only barely sweet. It makes a great dessert sauce option, though. For this recipe we take it easy, simply pairing saba with in-season berries or stone fruit, to highlight great ingredients.

1 cup whole fresh berries or pitted and sliced stone fruit (we suggest any combination of the following: blackberries, golden or yellow raspberries, pitted cherries, sliced white or mountain peaches, sliced plums or pluots, and/ or anything else you like)

⅓ cup saba

Combine the fruit in a bowl. Pour over the saba. Gently toss together to avoid bruising the fruit. Spoon over your favorite ice cream or sorbet.

This can be refrigerated in an airtight container for up to 2 days, but it's best when enjoyed immediately.

Ann's Granola

MAKES 2 QUARTS

Ann Grosz is a friend of ours who has a lovely home on Cape Cod. When we visit her, there's always a table full of food waiting for us. And when we get up in the morning, coffee, fruit, and granola are waiting for us. Her granola is just fantastic, and we thought about putting her on our staff just to make endless batches of it. But we love Ann too much to chain her to a stove, so instead we begged for the recipe.

2 cups rolled oats

½ cup wheat germ

½ cup whole bran

½ cup sunflower seeds

½ cup almonds, coarsely chopped in a food processor

¼ cup sesame seeds

¼ cup flaxseeds

¼ cup pumpkin seeds

¼ teaspoon ground cinnamon

6 tablespoons corn oil

6 tablespoons honey

⅔ teaspoon pure vanilla extract

½ cup golden raisins

½ cup dried cranberries

Arrange the oven racks in the upper and lower thirds of the oven. Preheat the oven to 325°F.

Combine the oats, wheat germ, bran, sunflower seeds, chopped almonds, sesame seeds, flaxseeds, pumpkin seeds, and cinnamon in a large mixing bowl. Set aside.

Heat the corn oil, honey, and vanilla in a small saucepan over medium heat for about 5 minutes, until warm and bubbly. Pour over the oat mixture and stir together until thoroughly incorporated.

Spread a thin layer of the granola mixture onto two ungreased baking sheets (if necessary, bake in batches). Bake for 10 to 15 minutes, until *"bien cuit"*—a nice dark golden brown. Remove from the oven and let cool on the sheets.

Crumble the granola into another large mixing bowl. Add the raisins and cranberries and toss together until thoroughly incorporated.

Spoon over your favorite ice cream or yogurt. Store for up to 2 weeks in airtight containers at room temperature.

COME AT ME BRO!

OTTAVIA

Toasted Curried Coconut
MAKES 2 CUPS

When you encounter dried coconut in a dessert, it's usually been presweetened. Those bags in the supermarket baking aisle are usually super-duper sweet, and we can't stand 'em. But unsweetened coconut often needs a partner-in-crime to amplify the taste, and in this case, you'll be helped out with some curry powder and a warm pan.

    We like to use finely shredded coconut, but larger flakes work fine. (Large flakes also make a great garnish for a salad or rice dish.) Since the taste of curry blends can vary widely, experiment with various brands.

2 cups unsweetened finely shredded coconut or coconut flakes

1 tablespoon mild yellow curry powder, or a bit more if necessary

Heat a large dry skillet over medium-low heat (do not use a nonstick skillet). Add the coconut. Sprinkle the curry powder on top, stir to coat the coconut, and cook until the coconut is golden brown, 8 to 10 minutes; stir often to avoid burning the coconut. Because of its density, shredded coconut will take longer to cook than coconut flakes. Be patient, and do not turn up the heat. Taste for seasoning and add more curry powder if necessary.

The coconut is best enjoyed immediately. We recommend pairing it with chocolate or ginger ice cream.

LICK IT!

Whiskey Walnuts

MAKES 2 CUPS

We knew we wanted a wet walnuts recipe—we were feeling nostalgic.
Doug took the lead on this one and knocked it out of the park. Consider
it the 1964 Triumph Bonneville motorcycle of wet walnuts.

1½ cups walnuts

½ cup dark corn syrup

¾ cup maple syrup

⅓ cup whiskey

Dash of coarse sea salt

Arrange an oven rack in the center of the oven. Preheat the oven to 275°F.

Scatter the walnuts on a baking sheet. Toast in the oven for 2 minutes. Toss and bake for another 2 minutes, or until they have just begun to brown. (Burnt walnuts taste very bitter, so it's better to err on the conservative side.) Remove the walnuts from the oven and let cool for 5 minutes. Roughly chop the walnuts (save that dusty powder) and set aside.

Heat the corn syrup and maple syrup in a medium saucepan over medium-low heat. Stir to combine, bring to a simmer, and simmer for about 8 minutes, stirring frequently. Add the whiskey. The mixture will foam up for a spell, but keep stirring. Add the sea salt and stir to combine. Allow the mixture to simmer for another 5 to 8 minutes, until it coats the back of a spoon. Remove from the heat and stir in the walnuts, including that powder. Allow to cool slightly—the mixture will be very hot!

Spoon the warm wet walnuts over your favorite ice cream and dig in! Store any leftovers in the refrigerator in an airtight container for up to 2 weeks; reheat before serving.

Pineapple & Mint

MAKES 1 QUART

This is one of Bryan's summer favorites. Like the granola (see page 45), it got its start during trips to our friend Ann's Cape Cod home. The strong acidic bite of pineapple is tempered by the cool, fresh mint. It's so refreshing on a hot day you can't help but close your eyes and imagine sitting outside watching the waves. You can turn this into a great fruit salad by using pineapple chunks instead of dice.

1 whole pineapple, peeled, cored, and diced

½ cup loosely packed fresh mint leaves, finely chopped

Toss the pineapple and mint together in a medium mixing bowl until the mint is evenly distributed.

Spoon over your favorite sorbet or into your favorite fruity cock- or mocktail.

Kiwi & Elderflower

MAKES ABOUT 1¼ CUPS

We imagine this is something Auntie Mame might have served her guests. After one hell of a party at Mame's place, where you'd chatted up Douglas Fairbanks Sr., Charles Demuth, and Ella Fitzgerald (and was that Dalí in the corner?), Mame was generous enough to let you crash in a spare room. Waiting for you when you woke, feeling a little hung, was some hair of the dog: a glass of bubbly with kiwi and elderflower floating in it. Downstairs, little Patrick was eating the exact same thing, but spooned over a heaping bowl of his favorite ice cream.

4 kiwis

¼ cup elderflower syrup

½ teaspoon grated lime zest (use a Microplane)

Cut the kiwis lengthwise in half. Scoop out the flesh from each half with a spoon (just like you would an avocado), keeping it in one piece. Place the halves flat side down on a cutting surface and slice into small cubes. Place in a small bowl, drizzle the elderflower syrup over the kiwi, and sprinkle with the lime zest. Gently toss until mixed together, being careful not to bruise or mash the fruit.

Spoon over your favorite sorbet or into your favorite fruity cock- or mocktail.

VARIATION: For a more hoity-toity version, use St-Germain, an elderflower liqueur, instead of the syrup.

SAUCES

Remember that time in tenth grade when you had that epiphany about loving gym class and an uncontrollable urge to try out for track & field? Neither do we. When we weren't glued to MTV or forced to go on the occasional band-camp trip, we would ride our bikes barefoot to our closest friend's place and pretend we were Julia Child (we both really did this). Our sauce section is devoted to the most luxurious of foods: ooey gooey, sweet, and sticky.

Bourbon Butterscotch

MAKES 1 QUART

We didn't really want to get into the butterscotch game after our experiences on the truck. It seemed like a topping best left to hypoglycemic junkies or career sugar addicts. After opening our shop, and distancing ourselves from the lousy commercial butterscotch available to ice cream truckers, we decided to give it a second look. It also helped that we had a case of bourbon. We didn't drink it all . . . we saved some for developing this recipe.

½ pound (2 sticks) unsalted butter

One 16-ounce box dark brown sugar (2¼ packed cups)

¼ cup dark corn syrup

1 cup heavy cream

½ teaspoon coarse sea salt

1 teaspoon pure vanilla extract

½ cup bourbon, plus a generous splash

Combine the butter, brown sugar, corn syrup, cream, salt, vanilla, and ½ cup bourbon in a large saucepan (using a large saucepan will help prevent the mixture from boiling over), and cook over medium-low heat, stirring frequently to prevent burning, until the sugar is completely dissolved (the sauce should not have any grit to it). Then cook, stirring, for another 15 minutes, or until the sauce has reduced and thickened; it should be a dark caramel color and thick enough to coat a spoon.

Remove from the heat and stir in the generous splash of bourbon, or to taste. If you have a heavy hand with your pour, who are we to judge? Let cool a bit, until warm, not hot, and gooey, not runny, then pour over ice cream. Eat and repeat.

Store refrigerated in an airtight container for up to 2 weeks; reheat and stir before using.

VARIATION: For a not-so-bourbon butterscotch, just leave out the bourbon. But if you do, angels will cry.

Why Do Sauces Go Crazy When I Add Alcohol to Them?

Doesn't *everything* go a little crazy when you add alcohol to it? Remember that time we made out that night at that bar after those shots? Yeah, I knew you were thinking the same thing.

Alcohol has a lower boiling point than most other liquids. That means it will transform from liquid into gas at a lower temperature. If you mix everything at room temperature and then heat it slowly, you won't see the same reaction as you would if you added the alcohol to a simmering sauce. If the sauce is just simmering (below the boiling point) and you add alcohol, it immediately turns into a gas, and the result can be quite violent. The taste will be left behind, but the alcohol itself usually evaporates within 20 to 30 seconds.

Orange-Tequila Caramel

MAKES 1 QUART

Once you have a great base recipe in your repertoire you realize you have the makings of countless variations. Such is the case with Bourbon Butterscotch (page 54), which we tweaked when we were participating in a "tacos and tequila" themed event to create this recipe. Swapping out the alcohol and adding some orange zest gives this version a whole new flavor profile. Now that we've given you two versions, it's your turn to come up with something!

½ pound (2 sticks) unsalted butter

One 16-ounce box light brown sugar (2¼ packed cups)

¼ cup light corn syrup

1 cup heavy cream

½ teaspoon coarse sea salt

1 teaspoon pure vanilla extract

½ cup tequila, plus a generous splash

1 tablespoon grated orange zest

Combine the butter, brown sugar, corn syrup, cream, salt, vanilla, and ½ cup tequila in a large saucepan (using a large saucepan will help prevent the mixture from boiling over), and cook over medium-low heat, stirring frequently to prevent burning, until the sugar is completely dissolved (the sauce should not have any grit to it). Then cook, stirring, for another 15 minutes, or until the sauce has reduced and thickened; it should be a dark caramel color and thick enough to coat a spoon.

Remove from the heat and stir in the orange zest and the generous splash of tequila, or to taste. Let cool a bit, until warm, not hot, and gooey, not runny, then pour over ice cream. Eat and repeat.

Store refrigerated in an airtight container for up to 2 weeks; reheat and stir before using.

VARIATION: Just like with the Bourbon Butterscotch, this recipe can work without the alcohol if desired.

C U Later Suckers

Dab Talbe

Dulce de Leche MAKES 3 CUPS

When asked by customers what dulce de leche is, we usually describe it as "caramel's milk-based cousin." Sweetened milk and a little vanilla are cooked at a very low temperature until the sugars caramelize and it has reduced to one-quarter (or less) of the starting volume.

The "long way" to make DDL (as it's known around our stores) will take you upward of five hours. There's a shortcut in which you boil a can of sweetened condensed milk, but that method turns us off for two reasons: you can't control the taste, and you risk an exploding can of scalding milk. Here's our compromise: we still start with sweetened condensed milk, but cook it opened (not in the can) in a double boiler so we can tweak the taste if necessary.

Two 14-ounce cans sweetened condensed milk (whole, low-fat, or nonfat)

½ teaspoon coarse sea salt

¼ teaspoon baking soda

⅛ teaspoon pure vanilla extract

Fill the bottom of a double boiler with water and bring to a simmer. Empty the cans of condensed milk into the double boiler insert and heat for 1 minute. Then whisk in the salt, baking soda, and vanilla, partially cover, and cook, stirring every 15 minutes, for 2 hours or so. Don't forget to check your water level—refill as necessary to keep it from boiling away. After about 2 hours, you should have a nice thick sauce that is ready to serve.

Store refrigerated in an airtight container for up to 2 weeks. Reheat before using if you want a warm, saucy consistency or use it cold as a thick spread.

Baking Soda in Dulce de Leche—What's the Point?

SCIENCE CLUB

Baking soda isn't *really* necessary to make a delicious dulce de leche, but it will produce a fuller, darker, smoother, more fabulous sauce, and that's what really matters. How does it do that?

Baking soda is a sodium bicarbonate—it's the same stuff they drank in *Mad Men* when they had indigestion. When you have too

much acid in your stomach, if you add something that is alkaline (the opposite of acidic), it will even everything out by balancing the pH level.

Adding baking soda to the condensed milk prevents the milk from curdling when it is heated. Without it, you may end up with a somewhat grainy texture after the mixture cools because the

milk proteins will stick together more. And with it, the dulce de leche will be a few shades darker, a result of the Maillard reaction. This is what causes your steak to turn brown when you grill it, and it's also responsible for that nice golden crust on your bagel. It's similar to caramelization but involves proteins instead of sugars.

Awesomesauce MAKES 1 QUART

This recipe began when Doug had a week with no bassoon work and an urge to make batches of chocolate something. Bryan won't stand for untweaked chocolate—it has to be smoky, or spicy, or salty—so for this particular recipe, we went spicy. This sauce was one of the first of our own recipes that made it onto Big Gay Ice Cream Shop's menu. Doug had just finished making a giant batch of what was then called "spicy chocolate sauce" when a text message blipped onto his phone. The message was from Stacy London and said simply, "You should name something on your menu Awesomesauce." Stacy's timing was impeccable, and that's how a woman famous for not cooking named one of our items. She probably tells people she wrote the recipe, bless her heart.

3 cups sugar

1½ cups whole milk

2 cinnamon sticks

6 tablespoons unsalted butter

½ cup plus 1 tablespoon unsweetened cocoa powder

1½ teaspoons coarse sea salt

1 teaspoon chipotle chili powder

½ teaspoon cayenne pepper

3 ounces semisweet chocolate

1½ teaspoons pure vanilla extract

Combine the sugar, milk, cinnamon sticks, and butter in a large saucepan and whisk vigorously over medium heat for 5 to 6 minutes, or until completely smooth. There should be no grittiness—all the sugar should be dissolved. Add the cocoa powder, salt, chili powder, cayenne, chocolate, and vanilla and stir until the chocolate is completely melted and incorporated; be sure to scrape the sides and bottom of the saucepan to avoid burning the chocolate. The sauce will be silky and have a nice sheen when ready. Remove the cinnamon sticks.

Taste-test before using, and adjust the spices if necessary. Let cool somewhat before spooning over ice cream.

Store refrigerated in an airtight container for up to 2 weeks. The leftover Awesomesauce is great reheated, for a sauce, and also good cold, as a rich, spicy spread.

VARIATION: For Not-So-Awesomesauce (meaning not spicy), leave out the chipotle and cayenne.

MOST LIKELY TO SUCCEED

Here's the thing, and I have always said this: gay ice cream tastes way better than any bullcockadoodie straight ice cream out there. So when I heard about the Big Gay Ice Cream Truck, I just thought, "Finally someone's got his hand on the switch." Doug and I connected on Twitter, aka my second home. We made plans for me to serve soft-serve in their truck for charity. Immediately, I started planning an outfit--sparkles, heels, very glam. I was beyond thrilled to do it, but a few things came up (like a hurricane and a broken heel) and we had to postpone.

In the meantime, I became obsessed with the idea of me as a dairy queen. I imagined myself in various looks making Bea Arthurs and American Globs with double chocolate. I get really excited about chocolate. I love it. I respect it. When I see chocolate abused, like a crushed M&M on the street, I mourn for it. So if I were going to serve ice cream, it'd have to be drenched in chocolate gold. That's when it hit me: I would serve a signature sauce. It'd be chocolate--and awesome. An awesomesauce. I texted Doug, "Put this on your menu: Awesomesauce. Chocolate. Spicy. Do it." Done. I put a giant checkmark next to "Make an important contribution to American ice cream culture" on my master to-do list. Thanks for that, Doug and Bryan! And remember: In ice cream and life, there is no such thing as too saucy.

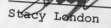

Stacy London

Banana-Cocoa Puree

MAKES 1½ CUPS

We are not usually fans of mixing fruit and chocolate, but neither of us can say no to bananas and chocolate. The bananas need to be seriously ripe and the skins should be brown, or the puree will take on a slightly bitter taste. If necessary, add a little sugar, tasting as you go, until you reach your desired sweetness. You may wonder about the addition of cayenne pepper, but don't worry, this isn't spicy. The cayenne just helps the flavors pop.

2 very ripe bananas, cut into 1-inch chunks

2½ tablespoons unsweetened cocoa powder

¼ teaspoon pure vanilla extract

¼ teaspoon cayenne pepper

Pinch of coarse sea salt

Sugar (optional)

Place the bananas, cocoa, vanilla, cayenne pepper, and sea salt in a blender and puree until smooth. If not sweet enough for your liking, add ½ teaspoon sugar and pulse. Repeat as necessary, but don't go overboard on the sweetness. Spoon over the ice cream of your choice.

Store refrigerated in an airtight container for up to 2 days.

Fig Sauce

MAKES 1 CUP

There's an ice cream joint in San Francisco's Mission District called Humphry Slocombe. If we tell you that the name of the place is culled from character names from the British TV series *Are You Being Served?* and that they have a taxidermied two-headed calf on the wall of the shop, you'll understand that Humphry Slocombe founder and chef Jake Godby is our kind of people.

Jake came to Los Angeles to help with our truck pop-up there. We wanted a fig sauce topping to pair with our favorite olive oil, so he contributed this great recipe. Jake is possibly insane and may drop off the grid one day soon. But for now, let's just enjoy the fact that he can cook. Really well.

¾ cup sugar

½ cup water

12 fresh Black Mission figs, quartered (do not use dried figs)

½ teaspoon kosher salt

1 tablespoon balsamic vinegar

1 tablespoon bourbon

1 teaspoon pure vanilla extract

Cook the sugar in a heavy-bottomed nonreactive saucepan over medium-high heat for about 10 minutes, until it starts to liquefy and turn a deep brown. Carefully stir in the water (beware of the spatter) to stop the sugar from burning.

Add the figs, reduce the heat, and continue to cook, stirring occasionally, for 2 to 3 minutes, until the figs start to fall apart. Add the salt, vinegar, bourbon, and vanilla, then puree in a blender. Spoon the sauce, either warm or cooled, over your choice of ice cream.

Store refrigerated in an airtight container for 1 week. Stir briskly before reusing; do not reheat.

THAT'S FRANK!
WE ♡ FRANK.

Frankensauce
MAKES 3 CUPS

In the summer of 2012, as we were thinking about introducing our truck to LA, we met Jon Shook and Vinny Dotolo. One of Jon and Vinny's restaurants is called Son of a Gun, and its previous chef, Frank Anderson (a Mainer like Doug), created a brilliant kimchi-esque sauce for their menu. Bryan adapted it into a great topping for ice cream, so if you like a little heat, this might become your new favorite thing. Thanks, Frank! Oh, yeah, and you other two.

1 cup kochukaru (Korean dried chili flakes)

One 1½-inch piece fresh ginger, peeled (scrape off the skin with a spoon)

1 medium carrot, peeled and chopped

1½ tablespoons sugar

1 cup water

1 cup Simple Syrup (page 141)

¼ cup rice vinegar

1½ teaspoons kosher salt

Add the chili flakes, ginger, carrot, sugar, water, simple syrup, vinegar, and salt to a blender and blend on high for 3 minutes, or until completely smooth. If you prefer a more refined sauce, pass through a sieve before using.

Spoon over your choice of ice cream. We definitely recommend putting this over something chocolatey.

Store refrigerated in an airtight container for 1 week. Stir briskly before serving.

CLASS STONERS

We had heard from a bunch of friends that we needed to meet the Big Gay Ice Cream guys. As luck would have it, we got an e-mail from them saying that they wanted to come out to LA and do an ice cream truck for a week, and did we want to meet them and possibly help them out. We agreed to meet them.

Doug and Bryan rolled into our restaurant Animal. They were both drinking Diet Cokes. You know how they say gay guys can talk? Well shit, they did. They told us the story of how they got started and they just kept going. Throughout the entire meeting, they kept pulling Diet Coke after Diet Coke out of Bryan's tote bag and pounding them like they were beers and we were all watching the Super Bowl. After about an hour, we started to feel like we were lifelong friends. We offered them the family meal, which happened to be chicken tacos. We weren't counting, but it looked like they each ate about ten. By taco eleven, we were helping them with their LA truck. At taco fifteen, we offered our guesthouses to the guys, not knowing they were a couple. They both crashed at Jon's house and Frank showed them around.

Their truck went live here during the time that Sandy hit NYC and fucked up their store. They showed a lot of strength and perseverance during that week, and while they did get stranded in LA for a couple of days, it gave us more time to get to know them. Only Bryan and Doug could be this big, this gay, and make ice cream this good!

(signature)

Jon Shook

(signature)

Vinny Dotolo

Blueberry-Balsamic Sauce

MAKES 3 CUPS

Doug is a Mainer, and Mainers are very vocal about only a few foods: Moxie, maple syrup, lobster, and blueberries. Maine blueberries are much smaller than their Cape Cod cousins, but they pack some serious flavor in their teeny packages. Our blueberry sauce recipe keeps Mainers happy by staying simple. We use just a little bit of lemon juice, which brightens up the blueberries and makes them taste even more delicious. We prefer this sauce cold over ice cream but warm over pancakes is great, too. We don't puree it, so there's plenty of lumpy berry goodness in the final product.

4 cups fresh or frozen blueberries

½ cup sugar

3 tablespoons balsamic vinegar

½ teaspoon grated lemon zest (use a Microplane)

Juice from ¼ lemon (approximately 1¾ teaspoons)

Combine the blueberries and sugar in a medium heavy-bottomed saucepan and bring to a simmer over medium heat. Do not boil. Smash the berries with a fork as they begin to simmer and pop. Continue cooking for another 5 minutes, or until the sugar is completely dissolved. Add the balsamic vinegar and simmer for another 7 to 10 minutes, stirring often. Remove from the heat and let the sauce cool for 10 minutes.

Add the lemon zest and lemon juice and stir to incorporate. Transfer to a covered container and refrigerate for 45 minutes, or until cold.

Stir before spooning over your choice of sorbet or ice cream.

Store refrigerated in an airtight container for up to 1 week; stir before serving.

Hot Fudge MAKES 1½ CUPS

Schrafft's lunch counters started around 1900 in Boston and by the middle of the century had a number of locations in New York City. It attracted a large crowd of single ladies and between-job Broadway actors to its counters. Combine this with their sponsorship of the annual telecasts of *The Wizard of Oz* and their inspiration for some of the best lines in *Auntie Mame* ("Patrick and I just stuffed ourselves at Schrafft's. Do you know what your silly nephew did? He spoke French to the counterman. Imagine anyone speaking French. To a counterman. At Schrafft's!") and you'll agree that Schrafft's might have been the original Big Gay Ice Cream Shop.

Our hot fudge recipe is spun from the one served at Schrafft's. Cooked right, it has a deeply dark and rich taste that turns ice cream into something otherworldly. It's from a hot fudge waterfall in a land where unicorns nibble on rainbow-colored cotton candy.

1 tablespoon unsweetened cocoa powder

1 cup sugar

¾ cup heavy cream

¼ cup light corn syrup

2 tablespoons unsalted butter

2 ounces unsweetened chocolate

1 teaspoon pure vanilla extract

Pinch of coarse sea salt

A few drops of malt vinegar

Whisk the cocoa, sugar, and ¼ cup of the heavy cream in a medium heavy-bottomed saucepan over medium heat until smooth. Add the corn syrup, butter, chocolate, and the remaining ½ cup cream and bring to a boil over medium heat, without stirring. Then cook for about 3 minutes longer, until a candy thermometer reaches 236°F. Remove from the heat.

Stir in the vanilla, salt, and malt vinegar. The sauce will thicken upon cooling or when poured over ice cream.

Store refrigerated in an airtight container for up to 2 weeks; reheat before serving.

Magical Shell MAKES 2 QUARTS

Chocolate shell recipes can seem like a science project disaster waiting to happen. After all, what sort of strange sorcery (and hodgepodge of chemicals) makes it harden on contact with ice cream anyway? Most versions use coconut oil (the same stuff your movie theater popcorn is popped in) and taste way too much like, well, daiquiris than chocolate sauce.

Behold Magical Shell from Jenn Louis, a seriously excellent chef and owner of two restaurants in Portland, Oregon, including Sunshine Tavern, where it's on the menu. Deceptively simple with only three ingredients, Jenn's recipe is a smart solution to getting rid of that coconut aftertaste (use olive oil instead) as well as the perfect ratio of ingredients to ensure a homemade version still turns into a shell. But the "magic" in this recipe isn't just that the chocolate hardens, it's that Jenn figured out a way to make both chocolate and ice cream taste better.

3¾ cups olive oil

3 pounds 60% bittersweet chocolate chunks or morsels

4 teaspoons coarse sea salt or kosher salt

Whisk the olive oil and chocolate in a medium heavy-bottomed saucepan over medium-low heat until smooth. Be careful not to scald the chocolate. Add the salt and continue whisking until thoroughly incorporated. Remove from the heat and let cool to room temperature before serving.

Ladle over your choice of ice cream and watch the magic happen.

Store in an airtight container at room temperature for up to 6 weeks. Do not store in the refrigerator. If the sauce hardens, warm gently by placing the container in warm water, stirring until pourable.

have a peachy
summer!
♡ Jenn
louis

Strawberry-Tarragon Sauce

MAKES 2 CUPS

Beware of bum berries! If you cut a strawberry in half and it's white inside, it might be fresh, but it's also pretty much useless. It's been "flash ripened" in a hothouse and will barely taste like anything. If strawberries are not in season, use frozen berries. They will be much tastier than those off-season frauds, and there is no need to thaw them ahead of time—just let them warm up in the pan first before adding the other ingredients.

1 pound fresh strawberries, hulled and sliced, or one 16-ounce bag frozen strawberries

¼ cup sugar

Pinch of coarse sea salt

1 tablespoon Grand Marnier

Grated zest of ½ lemon or orange (use a Microplane)

1 small bunch fresh tarragon, tied together

Combine the strawberries, sugar, and salt in a medium saucepan and bring to a simmer over medium heat. Do not boil. Smash the berries with a fork to break them apart. Continue cooking, stirring frequently, for 5 minutes, or until the sugar is completely dissolved.

Reduce the heat to low. Add the Grand Marnier, zest, and tarragon and heat, stirring often, for another 7 to 10 minutes. Remove the tarragon with a slotted spoon before serving. Let the sauce cool for at least 10 minutes. Serve warm over ice cream.

Store refrigerated in an airtight container for up to 1 week. Serve cold or reheat.

VARIATION: For a smoother sauce, add half the sauce to a blender and blend until smooth. Return the blended mixture to the saucepan and stir to incorporate.

Paulette goto
#1 plate licker (in public)
↳ super duper #1 fruit fly

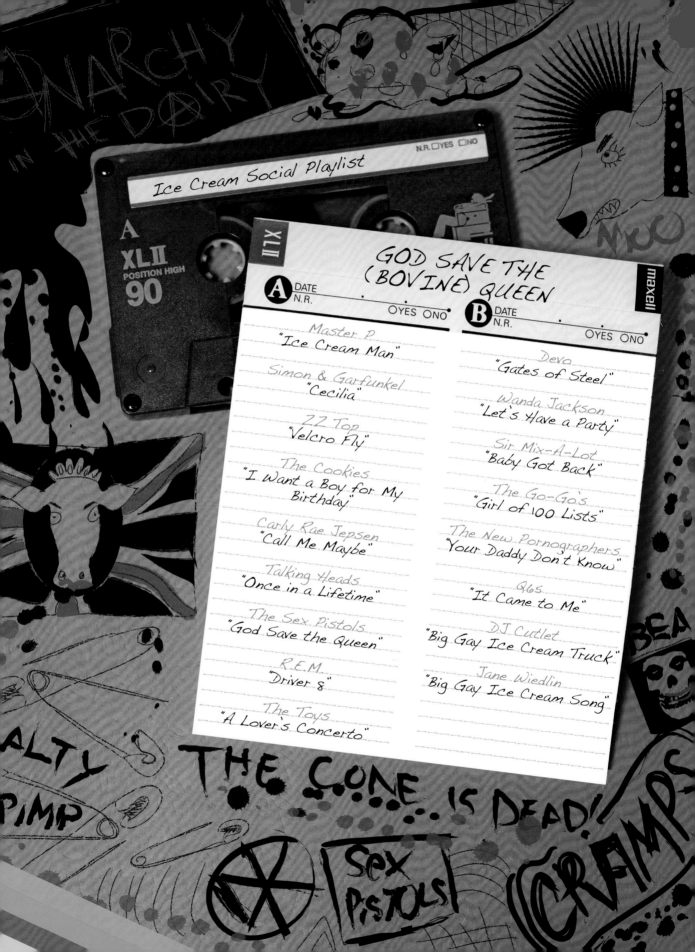

Junior Year

SOME ASSEMBLY REQUIRED— SUNDAES, FLOATS, AND SHAKES

SEX ED
The Saucier Side of Ice Cream

Sex, Drugs, and Sade

Ice cream: so wholesome, so evocative of childhood innocence, so, well, vanilla. Well, yes. You certainly can't argue with that. It's a mash-up of dessert and candy and sugary fun. It's for kids or the kid in all of us. Think cute, cuddly cows with big long eyelashes. Or the fantastical world of Willy Wonka (without the decapitated chicken projected in the tunnel scene). But in our line of work, sometimes ice cream is more than unicorns and rainbow sprinkles.

Take, for example, some of the items Doug found in ice cream trucks, so thoughtfully left behind by other drivers:

• Syringes, apparently used (though without needles)

• An aluminum softball bat

• A wooden baseball bat

• A switchblade

• Several dime bags (of marijuana)

• Joints

• Shake cups full of urine

• Condoms (still in their wrappers)

• Beer

• A white high-heeled shoe

• A sign for something called "The Salty Wimp"

• Ed Hardy T-shirts, Ed Hardy lighters, Ed Hardy air fresheners, Ed Hardy energy powder

• A Sade CD

• Handwritten poetry

Ice cream trucks, in other words, are not nearly as innocent as one might wish them to be. You're not that far off if you think of them as rolling dens of sin. We had heard stories about trucks being mobile pot stores, and apparently we weren't the only ones. On numerous occasions we were approached by eager pot seekers. Our truck was bone dry (at least once Doug tossed everything listed above out and put it through a Silkwood shower).

The truck certainly provided a kind of education. Sex education, to be specific. That first summer on the truck, Doug quickly realized he would be spending all his time standing two feet above his customers. It was an entirely new and unique vantage point. It was, in essence, an unending parade of cleavage. He couldn't help himself. After about two months of this, he caught himself staring down and apologized. "I'm sorry," he said, "but I've never really looked at breasts from this vantage before and just realized how prominently displayed they are from up here. And they're pretty great!" She was very flattered, and the friend with her agreed, saying, "They really are a lot of fun."

Confidence Ice Cream

So what is it about ice cream that gives it such a therapeutic quality? Ice cream really does seem to relax people, help them open up, and lead them to reveal themselves in the strangest ways. Sometimes literally, like the time a customer at the truck told Doug, "I have a really nice butt," and then showed it to him, right in the middle of Union Square. Or the time we were treated to a striptease, but one with a purpose that didn't involve us.

We were parked outside a bar in the East Village. Toward the end of our night, a woman sauntered up with a large purse and an even larger shopping bag and ordered a cone. As she was ordering it, she proceeded to undress. She took off her shirt, changing into a skimpier, sexier one pulled from her purse. Then she took off her sneakers and put on a pair of what we call "fuck-me pumps." She even managed to change from her jeans to a miniskirt, pulling the jeans off from underneath the skirt.

Midway through her striptease, we stopped her. As fascinating as it all was as a piece of street performance, we needed to know what on earth was going on. So she explained: she needed confidence ice cream. She was on her way to her boyfriend's workplace to break up with him, and the shopping bag held everything of his from her apartment. She had gone home from work, grabbed his clothes, put them in the

bag, grabbed herself a change of clothes, and run out the door. She admitted she hadn't really thought of where she'd end up changing her clothes. Obviously that didn't matter.

Doug asked if she was changing so that she'd look her best, and she said, "Exactly! I've got my look down, I've got my fuck-me pumps, and I'm going to show him what he's losing."

So we gave her a Monday Sundae. She told us she'd be back in an hour or so for a post-traumatic cone, but she never came back. We figured either they'd had break-up sex or she went to a bar for a post-traumatic drink instead.

But we loved the idea of confidence ice cream! Usually people think of ice cream as something to eat when they've been dumped, not when they're gathering the courage to dump someone else. It's labeled as a comfort food, a condolence food. There's a popular theory that a great way to hook up with someone is to hang around a supermarket ice cream freezer. Someone morose will come by, and you'll end up bedding them. And since they get laid instead of eating a whole tub of Breyer's, everyone wins!

As a corollary, we offer this observation: during our time manning the soft-serve machine, we've noticed that ice cream, particularly chocolate ice cream, holds more emotional significance for women than men. For example, when we first created the Monday Sundae, it was something to help drum up sales on slow Mondays—a crazy "everything but the kitchen sink" sundae only available one day a week. For those of you who don't know, the Monday Sundae is vanilla

...THEY ARE THE CLASSIC DEFINITION OF LOSER!

GRRRR, THEY JUST BURN ME UP, THOSE, THOSE DREAMERS. THEY THINK THEY'RE SO HOT TO TROT! JUST BECAUSE THEY HAVE A REAL LIVE UNICORN FOR A SCHOOL MASCOT.

UM, WELL, IT'S COOLER THAN OUR MASCOT...

WHAT'S NOT COOL ABOUT A NAKED MOLE RAT?

YOU GONNA FINISH THAT?

WHAT'LL YA HAVE TODAY, FELLAS?

I'M A GIRL.

I'LL HAVE A HOT FUDGE SUNDAE WITH EXTRA FUDGE.

DO YOU THINK YOU SHOULD?

YOU ALWAYS COMPLAIN THAT THE ICE CREAM DOESN'T HAVE THE PROPER VISCOSITY, AND THE HOT FUDGE IS MORE LIKE COLD MUD...

I DO NOT!

LOOK AT THEM, ORDERING FOOD LIKE THEY DESERVE NOURISHMENT.

YEAH! THOUGH TECHNICALLY, SHAYE, THE HUMAN BODY REQUIRES NUTRIENTS.

THEY'RE NOT HUMAN. THEY'RE DREAMERS!

THIS ICE CREAM DOESN'T HAVE THE PROPER VISCOSITY.

AND THE HOT FUDGE IS MORE LIKE COLD MUD.

THAT'S THE FUDGE PACKERS' MOTTO, BOYS!

IF ONLY THE FUDGE PACKER BROTHERS WERE STILL AROUND. THEY DIED AND LEFT ME IN CHARGE. AND I'M RETIRING TO FLORIDA NEXT TUESDAY. THERE'S NO "NEXT GENERATION" TO TAKE OVER, IT'S SAD.

WHO CARES ABOUT THEIR STUPID UNICORN? I NEED TO GET OVER THIS GROIN PULL AND GET BACK IN THE GAME!

DRECK! DRECK! DRECK! DRECK!

UNICORNS *ARE* SAID TO HAVE MAGICAL HEALING POWERS...

MARCY — WHAT KIND OF POWERS?

WELL, SPECIFICALLY, THEIR HORN — KNOWN AS AN ALICORN — IS SAID TO CURE ALL KINDS OF AILMENTS. MEASLES, RUBELLA, EVEN LEPROSY.

WHAT ABOUT CYSTIC ACNE?

YOUR PIMPLES CAN WAIT, ALBIE! WE'VE GOT A GROIN TO HEAL.

HI GUYS! SO GOOD TO SEE YOU!

WHO IS SHE TALKING TO?

PROBABLY *MOI.*

HEY LADIES...

MY FRIENDS AND I WERE JUST WONDERING IF WE COULD BORROW YOUR UNICORN?

SHE SERIOUS?

UM, BORROW MISTY, THE SCHOOL MASCOT? I DON'T THINK SO. YOU'D PROBABLY MAKE LASAGNA OUT OF HER.

HAHA, DON'T BE SILLY — I DON'T EAT. WE JUST WANT HER TO HEAL DRECK'S GROIN INJURY SO HE CAN PLAY FOOTBALL AGAIN

CREEPY.

NO, IT'S JUST THAT UNICORN HORNS HAVE HEALING POWERS. AND DRECK'S GROIN IS TORN.

EWW.

OH, COME ON! YOU LOVE *GORY DETAILS.*

THERE WAS JUST SOMETHING SO AESTHETICALLY UNPLEASANT ABOUT THE SENTENCE "DRECK'S GROIN IS TORN."

WHEN A MAN'S GROIN IS TORN HE NEEEEEEEED TO GET TOUCHED BY A HORN, TONIGHT...

and chocolate ice creams, dulce de leche, sea salt, and whipped cream, all crammed into a Nutella-lined waffle cone. Eventually it just became too popular to limit to Mondays. Tons of women would show up after work or the gym or during a particularly sensitive time of month for them and order it for dinner. And we've learned from experience that when two women come in together and order it, there's no way in hell they want to split it. No ma'am. They each want their own.

Perhaps it's because ice cream can inspire such a personal and sometimes emotional reaction that we often find ourselves acting as a kind of ersatz shrink to customers who haven't had the best day. When we parked at Union Square, people would show up on their lunch break with their shoulders hiked up to their ears and their faces locked in a frown. Doug always enjoyed saying, "Look, before I hand you this, you need to drop your shoulders, take a deep breath, loosen your face, and, for the duration of this cone, don't think about any of that shit. Just think about the ice cream cone and enjoy it." And they'd always say, "You're right," and relax and wander off. The ice cream really did help.

Ice Cream & the Single Girl

Although being in the ice cream trade has made us unwitting magnets for characters with a flexible definition of the law, it's also made us unwitting accomplices to lesser and way more enjoyable crimes.

Perhaps our favorite to date is the story of a nice young woman who very frequently came to our truck. Sometimes she even came twice a day.

She always got the same thing—a Bea Arthur. A Bea is a vanilla cone with dulce de leche and crushed-up vanilla wafer cookies. This was back before it occurred to Doug that he could grind up the cookies in a food processor. He just beat the box with a metal shake cup, and the cookies were busted into chunks, not ground to dust.

One day this woman showed up and told Doug she had a story for him. It seems that she and her husband had agreed to go on a diet, and she was supposed to have been on it for the past two weeks. "But," she told Doug, "I kind of got caught cheating with you." One night, she was getting ready for bed and took off her shirt. "How's that diet going?" her husband asked. "Great!" she said. "What'd you have today?" her husband asked. "Just salad," she replied. "Then why," he asked, "is there a giant piece of cookie in your bra?" And he reached into her cleavage and procured a chunk of Nilla wafer.

MARY ALICE, ONCE A CAKE STAR AND ALWAYS OUR BFF

"Well," Doug said after he'd stopped laughing, "I guess I'm going to have to call you Cookie Tits from now on!" "Yes," she said, "you probably should." Years later, Cookie Tits still visits us.

Bea Mine ♥

Rest assured, things aren't always quite so saucy in our line of work. Sometimes we even see expressions of human emotion that are downright sweet, like the marriage proposals we've witnessed.

The first one happened at Union Square: the couple ordered and then, without warning the guy dropped to his knee and proposed. The girl started crying, and Doug was left holding a couple of slowly melting ice cream cones.

The second one happened when Doug was parked in Midtown. A guy came to the truck and told Doug he was supposed to meet his girlfriend there in fifteen minutes. He asked Doug to slip a ring (a fake one, just in case it ended up being ingested) on the end of the cone his lady friend ordered. When the time came, Doug gave the guy his cone first (something he never does—ladies first!), and then gave the girl her cone. When she saw the ring, she immediately burst into tears. He was already on one knee, and she just lost it. It was awesome.

The third proposal was at the East Village store. A guy contacted us about a week ahead of time and wanted us to put a specials sign on the counter that said something like, "Today's special is the Will You Marry Me, Joan?" As they looked at the menu, we would suggest the special, and she'd weep tears of joy. We were all prepared to play our parts, but when the couple came in, the guy was so nervous that he all but immediately fell on his knee and proposed. He missed his lines, and we missed our cues. His girlfriend was so confused. He repeated the question. She looked at us. We were standing there a tad lost and could only show her the sign, but she continued to be genuinely baffled. It all happened so fast. Finally we had to tell her that yes, he really was proposing. We were hoping she'd be emotional after learning what was really going on, but she was very nonchalant. "Sure, I will." They left pretty quickly after that, and we were like, "Well, that was weird. . . ."

Them's Fightin' Words

And then there were the fights.

Strangely enough, our fear of physical harm has never come from the numerous junkies we've encountered—or drunks, or cops, or pimps, or mysterious mafioso types brandishing guns (yes, there have been a few of those). Instead, fear of getting a bloody nose or a black eye came from where we'd least expected it: our brothers in arms in the food industry.

The two most heated encounters both occurred during summer food festivals on Governors Island. The pressure of long lines and large-scale events, the summer heat, and the isolation of the island seem to easily combine into a volatile mix. So much so that we have since boycotted doing any event on that island.

Most food events are assisted by volunteers.

In fact, volunteers are really the backbone of any such large-scale event. Most are amazing and extremely helpful. During one such event we did, there was a group of volunteers from a local culinary school. The pressure of food festivals is something culinary students should be able to master with a calm head. After all, they can't be worse than a fast-paced restaurant kitchen.

However, one volunteer kept bothering and antagonizing our friends who were manning our tables. He kept belittling us, our crew, and our menu. After getting nowhere with our friends, he got belligerent. That's when Bryan stepped in. He started calm, reminding the fellow that he needed to stop asking for things we didn't have and promising those things to the VIPs. He needed to consult the menu and ensure that the VIPs knew what was available and what wasn't. He needed to stop hounding our crew as they tried desperately to keep up with the line of hundreds of people in front of them.

But he didn't stop, and finally Bryan's temper got the best of him. Immediately the volunteer got up in Bryan's face, sweating and twitching, and tried to antagonize him into throwing the first swing. Being a little hotheaded himself, Bryan egged him on. Staring into his mad, twitching eyes, Bryan kept repeating, "Is this what you want to do? Do you want to hit me? Well, go ahead, hit me. What's the matter? Do it. Hit me. Because if you do—one of us is going to get kicked off this island and it won't be me." Dramatic pause. The dude walked off in a huff. But Bryan was true to his word. One of them was immediately kicked out of the event and off the island, and it wasn't Bryan.

The second encounter didn't involve a young and immature volunteer, but the volatile chef of one of NYC's most prominent—and some may say best—pizzerias. What is it about being on an island that makes tempers rise? After a successful all-day event, we closed up the truck and rolled into position to leave, waiting for the island security staff to usher us to the ferry. Security had told us to wait—under no circumstances were we to roll the truck unaccompanied (under penalty of permanent eviction from the island). A fellow vendor came over and asked us to come jump-start his vehicle, so we said that as soon as our escort returned, we'd be right over to help. That wasn't good enough—he flipped out. We were "pussies!" he exclaimed. Not only that, but we should "just go ahead and grow vaginas." The topper? "I wish there weren't all these people around so I could just kick the living shit out of you." Um, what? We were just standing here and then this?

It was all so absurd that we could do nothing but laugh in his face—and that really didn't go down well. The festival staff forced him back to his corner, and a few days later we got an apology e-mail that read along the lines of, "Your window got in the way of my baseball, so it broke, and mom said I had to tell you I'm sorry." Dude, we're all grown-ups. We're all working in the same field. WTF? Next time, either treat us like colleagues or come up with a better plan of attack: learn to read like a proper queen, and throw in some finger snaps. That's what gets us shaking in our Pradas!

DRAMA QUEEN

I don't know how I found Big Gay
Ice Cream on Twitter, but it was
meant to be. I like soft-serve, I
like the Village, and I like gays.
But, alas, I have been marooned in
Los Angeles for the last six years
working for Walt Disney. When I
saw that they were COMING TO LA IN
A FOOD TRUCK!!! it was a wet dream
come true. And what could be more
subversive than the Big Gay Ice
Cream Truck on the Disney lot in
Burbank, California, I ask you?

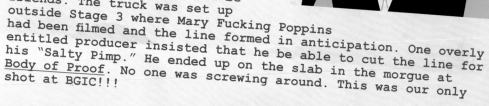

For my first meeting outside my
trailer with Doug and Bryan, I
was wearing no makeup and in full
curler mode. Doug said, "Not what
I was expecting" in his snarky
way and I knew we would all be
friends. The truck was set up
outside Stage 3 where Mary Fucking Poppins
had been filmed and the line formed in anticipation. One overly
entitled producer insisted that he be able to cut the line for
his "Salty Pimp." He ended up on the slab in the morgue at
Body of Proof. No one was screwing around. This was our only
shot at BGIC!!!

Once you've had a "Salty Pimp" there is no going back. I've
also learned there is no getting rid of BGIC. Doug and Bryan
won't leave me the fuck alone! On a promotional trip to NYC,
they surprised me at VH1 with a "Ryan Gosling" made with maple
syrup and Gosling rum, knowing my obsession with the young
man. Although I highly doubt he could taste half as good.

They next showed up when I was on Anderson Live and outed
him with a "Bea Arthur." He has now switched to rainbows and
unicorns at BGIC near his Village home. Subversive activists,
one cone at a time.

Warning: Big Gay Ice Cream will turn you. And you'll like it.

Dana Delany
Dana Delany

SUNDAES

What's a sundae? It may seem like a simple question, but there's a difference between a sundae and straight-up ice cream with a topping, and it's not just about whipped cream. Our personal definition is that it has to have both a crunchy and a gooey component to qualify. After that, whipped cream is just gravy (although our sundaes never go without it).

We "parfait" our sundaes, assembling them in layers, like this:

- a squirt or drizzle into the bowl of some of the gooey element,

- a scoop of ice cream,

- a bit more gooey and some crunchy,

- a repeat of all these layers,

- whipped cream around the top,

- and a garnish of a final touch of the crunchy

Feel free to use store-bought ice cream for our sundae recipes. It's only junior year, after all—a little cheating is expected. For those of you who fancy themselves advanced students and have an ice cream maker, follow our ice cream recipes in the Senior section (pages 126–175).

Mermaid Sundae SERVES 1

The Mermaid Sundae originated when we teamed up with New York City's Mermaid Inn. The seafood restaurant doesn't offer a dessert selection per se—only complimentary demitasses of chocolate pudding and a fortune-telling fish. So they asked us to be their dessert option on special occasions, and we came up with The Mermaid. For Bryan, seafood means Florida, Florida means the Keys, the Keys mean Key limes, and Key limes mean Key lime pie. This sundae is essentially Key lime pie à la mode. What is Key lime curd? Think of it like custard: sugar, eggs, butter, and fruit juice are cooked until thick and then allowed to set, and there you have curd. Fear not.

3 tablespoons Key lime curd

2 large scoops Vanilla Ice Cream (page 157) or Sweet Cream Ice Cream (page 147 or 156)

½ cup loosely packed broken-up graham cracker pie crust

Whipped Cream to garnish (optional; recipe follows)

Squirt (or spoon and swirl) 1 tablespoon of the lime curd into the bottom of your ice cream bowl. Add 1 scoop of ice cream. Add half of the remaining curd, squirting or drizzling it over the ice cream. Shower half of the grahams over that. Add the second scoop of ice cream, then add the remaining curd and grahams, repeating the previous step. Finish with the whipped cream, if using, squirting it around the sundae like a cone around a humiliated puppy's neck.

Whipped Cream MAKES 1 CUP

There are very few desserts that aren't improved by a nice dollop of freshly whipped cream. If you spring for really-high-grade cream, you may not even want to add the sugar or vanilla.

½ cup cold heavy cream

1 tablespoon confectioners' sugar

¼ teaspoon pure vanilla extract

Pour the cream into a chilled small bowl. Add the sugar and vanilla. Beat with an electric mixer on high until stiff peaks form, about 2 minutes. Store refrigerated in an airtight container for up to 2 days. Whisk again before serving.

Gobbler Sundae SERVES 1

We think about pie pretty much all day, every day. As a matter of fact, we're doing it right now and will again in about six minutes. The only thing that improves a great piece of pie is putting some ice cream on top, and during the truck's first summer, we decided to flip that around. How about some great ice cream with pie on top? *Glace à la tarte* perhaps? First came the Pumpkin Gobbler, then the Apple Gobbler, and finally the Mermaid (page 88).

FOR THE PUMPKIN GOBBLER

⅓ cup pumpkin butter

¼ cup maple syrup

FOR THE APPLE GOBBLER

⅓ cup apple butter

¼ cup Bourbon
   Butterscotch
   (page 54)

FOR ASSEMBLY

2 large scoops Vanilla
   Ice Cream (page 157)
   or Sweet Cream Ice
   Cream (page 147 or 156)

½ cup loosely packed
   broken-up piecrust
   (store-bought is fine),
   toasted in the oven

   Whipped Cream to
   garnish (optional;
   page 88)

Squirt (or spoon and swirl) one-quarter of the fruit butter into the bottom of your ice cream bowl. Add 1 scoop of ice cream. Add half of the remaining fruit butter and half of its accompanying syrup or sauce, squirting or drizzling it over the ice cream. Shower half of the piecrust pieces over that. Add the second scoop of ice cream, then add the remaining fruit butter, sauce, and piecrust pieces. Finish with whipped cream around the top like an Elizabethan collar, if you like.

HOMECOMING QUEEN

Like the start of so many passionate seductions, I first met the Salty Pimp on a crowded New York street corner. It was October 2010. The air was just turning from humid and sticky to cool and crisp. I was on the prowl for something sweet. The attraction between us was instantaneous, and I knew I could never resist: That cool, creamy center, oozing with gooey, golden caramel and sprinkled with just a hint of saline surprise. That rich and foreboding exterior, which echoed of dark powers and too much pleasure. All I dreamed of was for his flavors to engulf me, to ravage me to my core. The first taste of the Salty Pimp didn't disappoint. Even years later, although our meetings are sporadic, I know he will always satisfy my needs. Just knowing he is out there, available to me day or night, makes my heart race.

Gail Simmons

Gail Simmons

Salty Pimp Sundae SERVES 1

If you know us, you probably know the Salty Pimp—it's far and away our biggest-selling cone. We joke that this is the one that will put our grandchildren through college (fingers crossed that we don't have any grandchildren). Eating dinner on the truck is a luxury that doesn't happen much, so for Bryan, dinner often turned into crafting a sundae while standing and rocking around in the back of the truck as Doug drove it back to the depot. This sundae is the Salty Pimp in cup form, with the added pop and crunch of some crushed peanuts or cashews. It has pretty much everything: sweet and salty, creamy and sticky, smooth and crunchy, and, of course, gooey, too.

¼ cup Dulce de Leche (page 57)

2 large scoops Vanilla Ice Cream (page 157) or Sweet Cream Ice Cream (page 147 or 156)*

¼ cup Not-So-Awesomesauce (page 59)

¼ cup crushed peanuts or cashews

Coarse sea salt

Whipped Cream to garnish (optional; page 88)

*A number of ice cream flavors work well with the Salty Pimp. Try chocolate, coconut, or coffee too.

Squirt (or spoon and swirl) one-quarter of the dulce de leche into the bottom of your ice cream bowl. Add 1 scoop of ice cream. Add half of the remaining dulce de leche and half of the Not-So-Awesomesauce, squirting or drizzling them over the ice cream. Sprinkle half of the nuts and a little sea salt over that. Add the second scoop of ice cream, then add the remaining dulce de leche, sauce, and nuts, repeating the previous step. Finish with another sprinkle of sea salt and whipped cream, if using, squirting it around the sundae like the tiara on a children's pageant winner.

JAKE PIMPING OUT A CONE.

Ray-Ray Sundae SERVES 1

During our first year, we had tons of print and online press coverage, but very little, if any, TV coverage. We were told point-blank by many networks and TV shows that Middle America wouldn't respond favorably to us. That all changed with *The Rachael Ray Show*. Rachael's team didn't let any of those fears or concerns stop them, and Rachael saw us like we saw ourselves: quirky, fun, and whimsical. Rachael's favorite of the sundaes we made for the show was this one. So when it came time to naming it, Ray-Ray seemed only natural.

¼ cup Fig Sauce
(page 63)

2 large scoops Vanilla
Ice Cream (page 157)
or Sweet Cream Ice
Cream (page 147 or 156)

2 tablespoons high-
quality extra-virgin
olive oil

¼ cup toasted pine nuts

Coarse sea salt

Squirt (or spoon and swirl) one-quarter of the fig sauce into the bottom of your ice cream bowl. Add 1 scoop of ice cream. Add half of the remaining fig sauce and half of the olive oil, squirting or drizzling them over the ice cream. Shower half of the pine nuts over that. Add the second scoop of ice cream, then add the remaining fig sauce, olive oil, and pine nuts, repeating the previous step. Finish with a sprinkling of sea salt. Then mix it up a bit before you enjoy.

TESTIMONIAL

CLASS PUNSTER

Food in general is all about love. No haters allowed! I celebrate my Big Gay team for creating the most delicious thing since my own husband. It's not a Fig Newton of your imagination. It's real and it's legal. Try the best fig ice cream sundae, the ice cream of your dreams! I love you guys!

Peace, love, and sundaes forever.

Rachael Ray

P.S. My middle name is Sunday (*Domenica*).

Nuclear Winter Sundae SERVES 1

When people ask what's the weirdest thing we make, we point to this sundae. Doug's a real wimp when it comes to spicy food, but one day he realized that pairing spice with frozen dairy made eating it possible. For this recipe, we've taken an adventurous kitchen sink approach to layering various levels of spice and texture. The authentic, verified Nuclear Winter from the truck included a half-sour pickle spear on the side. Just try it. Trust us, no one ever said no to the pickle.

3 tablespoons Awesomesauce (page 59)

2 tablespoons Frankensauce (page 64) or Sriracha sauce

2 large scoops Chocolate Ice Cream (page 149)

2 tablespoons toasted unsweetened shredded coconut

¼ cup candied nuts

A pickle spear of your choosing to garnish

Squirt (or spoon and swirl) one-quarter of the two sauces into the bottom of your ice cream bowl. Add 1 scoop of ice cream. Add half of the remaining sauces, squirting or drizzling them over the ice cream. Shower half of the coconut and nuts over that. Add the second scoop of ice cream, then add what's left of the two sauces, coconut, and nuts, repeating the previous step. Finish by sticking the pickle spear into the side of the sundae like an intrusion, a thumb in your eye, an arrow in Saint Sebastian's side.

You taught me how to swallow the best of "CREAM". & I can't wait for our creamy SUMMER! Here's to PIE! — ALL TYPES! Claire Robin

American Globs Sundae SERVES 1

After having a bit of fun with the author Neil Gaiman on Twitter over whether "homosexual ice cream" could even exist, we got a last-minute notice that he was in New York City and about to make his first visit to our truck. Time wasn't on our side. Bryan ran out and came back with a bag of broken-up homemade pretzels from the farmers' market. We smashed the broken pieces into the ice cream, salted it up, and dipped it into chocolate. The whole thing looked like one big glob. Glob . . . globs . . . gods . . . Neil's *American Gods*. . . . We quickly wrote up a specials sign, and the American Globs was born.

¼ cup Magical Shell
   (page 70)

2 large scoops Vanilla
   Ice Cream (page 157)
   or Sweet Cream Ice
   Cream (page 147 or 156)

½ cup crushed large hard
   pretzels (not skinny
   pretzels)

   Sea salt

   Whipped Cream to
   garnish (optional;
   page 88)

Squirt (or spoon and swirl) one-quarter of the Magical Shell into the bottom of your ice cream bowl. Add 1 scoop of ice cream. Add half of the remaining shell, squirting or drizzling it over the ice cream. Shower half of the pretzels over that. Add the second scoop of ice cream, then add the remaining shell and pretzels, repeating the previous step. Finish with a sprinkle of sea salt and the whipped cream, if using.

CLASS GOTH

At the beautiful Amanda Palmer's New Year's Eve gig in Boston with the Boston Pops, the night before I proposed marriage to her, the night before she accepted, I was approached backstage by one of the woodwind players. He mentioned a mutual friend and gave me his own Twitter ID, BigGayIceCream. I must have looked bemused, because he went on to explain that he really did have an ice cream truck, in the summer, not at New Year's Eve, and that I should come and have an ice cream there.

So I did. I waited until it was summer. I followed Doug's Twitter feed to find out where the truck was, I went there, and I lined up. I got to the front of the line, and I completely failed to order an ice cream. "You are going to have an AMERICAN GLOBS," I was informed.

The American Globs had been created mere moments before. I am still not entirely certain that it was not invented at the moment I reached the front of the line. Crushed pretzels were involved (the pretzel, that most New York and confusing of foods) and liquid chocolate. The challenge involved was eating it while not covering oneself entirely in chocolate. (This was a prototype.)

Soon after, we were joined by the beautiful Amanda Palmer, with the almost-as-beautiful Brian Viglione in tow, both of the Dresden Dolls. More big gay ice creams were eaten. The second round of American Globs was less drippy than the first, although just as tasty.

A year later, (the even-more-beautiful-than-Brian-Viglione) Molly Crabapple made a poster for the Big Gay Ice Cream Truck, showing Mr. Wednesday, from _American Gods_, urging people to eat their American Globs. By now the American Globs had been perfected and was very unlikely to drip chocolate all over the person eating it--which I am not certain is a good thing.

Good food should carry some risk, after all. And you need to suffer, just a little, for those moments of perfect joy.

Neil Gaiman

FLOATS

Floats are a real bitch to make with soft-serve ice cream, so make your floats with hard-packed ice cream. Making one is easy: Fill a pint glass halfway with your soda of choice, then gingerly drop in one or two scoops of ice cream. It's best if you freeze your glasses for at least 30 minutes prior to assembling the floats.

A few of our favorite combinations:

• Sprecher's Root Beer with vanilla ice cream

• Mexican Coca-Cola with vanilla ice cream

• Orange Fanta with one scoop of orange sherbet and one of vanilla ice cream

• Grape Crush with one scoop of rainbow sherbet and one of vanilla ice cream

• Guinness beer with chocolate or coffee ice cream

• Izze lime soda (not lime seltzer) with a scoop of vanilla ice cream and a few drizzles of elderflower syrup for a decadent finish (or booze it up with an elderflower liqueur like St-Germain)

SCIENCE CLUB

Why Does Carbonated Soda Go Apeshit When Ice Cream Is Added to It?

Let's first discuss why carbonated soda foams at all. "Carbonated" means that carbon dioxide gas has been dissolved in the soda. *"Duh, everyone knows that!"* you say. *"We can see the bubbles, after all."* Well, in reality, if the gas were actually dissolved, you wouldn't see any bubbles. It's like when sugar is dissolved in a liquid—you can no longer see the sugar.

So, then, why can you see bubbles? Carbon dioxide gas actually likes being a gas and prefers that to being dissolved in a liquid. It doesn't take much encouragement: any little thing that attracts its attention will cause it to leave the liquid and turn into bubbles. The change in pressure when you open a can of soda does this. Pouring the soda into a glass does this. Adding ice does this. Adding sugar *really* does this (don't try that at home unless you have help to clean up a sticky mess). If you've ever seen the Mentos/Diet Coke YouTube videos, you know that the combination can be like detonating a bomb!

In other words, anything that is not already a liquid will cause carbon dioxide to leave the liquid and reclaim its preferred status. This is called nucleation. It requires a little something to start the reaction, and air is the best way to do that. Ever blow bubbles into your fountain drink? It causes a lot more bubbles!

Ice cream has A LOT of air in it—that's what gives it a soft, light texture, and that's what causes the explosion of bubbles when it's combined with soda. If you add soda to your ice cream, you will get a much grander eruption than if you add ice cream to your soda. This is because if you pour the soda into the glass first, a lot of the carbon dioxide will have formed bubbles and popped by the time you add the ice cream. If you add the ice cream to the glass first, there will actually be more bubbles when you add the soda.

Ice cream also has thickeners and fats in it—that's what causes the foam in a float. Basically, the outside of the bubbles are more stable and so they don't pop like normal bubbles. Cheers!

Mexican
Coke

Orange
Fanta

Grape
Crush

Guinness
Beer

Izze
Lime

Sprecher's
Root Beer

Black & White Shake

MAKES 2 THICK 8-OUNCE SHAKES

The Black & White Shake may be basic, but it is also a gold standard. The ingredients are three of the staples in any ice cream shop, and also three things you're likely to have at home: vanilla ice cream (the "white"), milk, and chocolate syrup (the "black"). That's it. Only the smallest amount of chocolate syrup is needed to punch through and create a really robust shake. Don't fight it—black-and-white it!

There are folks out there who feel very strongly about what brand of chocolate syrup makes the quintessential Black & White. Most old-school New Yorkers say it has to be Fox's U-Bet brand. But, good lord, it's chocolate syrup. It's coming from a squeeze bottle. Just use what's in your cupboard, people.

¾ cup whole milk

1 tablespoon chocolate syrup (or a big squirt if using a squeeze bottle)

4 large scoops Vanilla Ice Cream (page 157) or Sweet Cream Ice Cream (page 147 or 156)

Add the milk and chocolate syrup to a blender, cover, and quickly pulse the blender to combine. Add the ice cream, cover, and blend (on medium or "blend" setting, depending on your blender's vernacular) until you see a whirlpool form—that's when you know it's done. Any longer and you have ice cream soup. Pour or spoon the shake into two tall glasses. Top with any garnish you'd like—cherries, whipped cream, cacao nibs, foie, it's all good. Serve with straws and spoons. Mazel tov!

NOTE: If using store-bought ice cream, avoid vanilla *bean*.

Vanilla Shake

MAKES 2 THICK 8-OUNCE SHAKES

The simplest items can be the hardest. When you're dealing with only two or three ingredients, you'd better be damn sure to get it right. The vanilla shake is the Amanar of the ice cream world. It's a roundoff onto the springboard, back handspring onto the horse, and one-and-a-half flips with two-and-a-half twists right into the glass. Bring it on!

¾ cup whole milk

4 large scoops Vanilla Ice Cream (page 157)

Add the milk and ice cream to a blender, cover, and blend on a medium setting until you see a whirlpool form—that's when you know it's done. Pour or spoon the shake into two tall glasses. Top with any garnish you'd like—cherries, whipped cream, shaved chocolate, 'shrooms, it's all good. Serve with straws and long-handled spoons. Dig it!

A NOTE ABOUT BLENDERS

If you are a soda fountain purist, you might want to invest in what is called a milk shake or malted machine. These machines were the predecessor of blenders, and they are still the gold standard at any place that makes a "real" milk shake. They have a spinning stem that, when lowered into the metal cup of ice cream, syrup, and milk, mixes and aerates the ingredients. Most modern blenders are designed to crush, destroy, and kill. As such, they will completely liquefy your shake if you're not careful (especially high-end brands such as Vitamix). Sure, you can make a decent shake in any blender, but you've got to be mindful of what the sucker is capable of doing.

Ginger-Curry Shake

MAKES 2 THICK 8-OUNCE SHAKES

The Ginger-Curry Shake was the first specialty shake of our own devising to find a regular spot on the menu. We'd been using The Ginger People's ginger syrup as an ice cream topping, encouraging people to give it a sprinkling of curry powder as a complement. Kyle, one of our regular customers, asked if we'd consider making that as a shake. With him as our guinea pig, we set about getting it right. Curry powder is a blend of spices, so you never know exactly what you may get until trying the end result. Start with the amount listed below and go from there.

¾ cup whole milk

¼ cup ginger syrup

⅛ teaspoon mild yellow curry powder

4 large scoops Vanilla Ice Cream (page 157) or Sweet Cream Ice Cream (page 147 or 156)

Add the milk, ginger syrup, and curry powder to a blender, cover, and quickly pulse the blender to combine. Add the ice cream, cover, and blend on a medium setting until you see a whirlpool form—that's when you know it's done. Pour or spoon the shake into two tall glasses. Top with any garnish you'd like—candied lime rind, whipped cream, a drizzle of more ginger syrup, it's all good. Serve with straws and spoons. Chock dii!

HICCUP ALERT: We've liquored up this shake to good results. Reduce the amount of milk to ½ cup and use ¼ cup well-chilled rum or coconut-flavored alcohol. New York City food personality Eddie Huang showed up one night with a bottle of coconut-infused vodka, and we used some in this shake. From what we remember (that night has grown hazy over time), it tasted excellent! We always keep our liquor bottles in the freezer, and we assume you do the same.

"What a long strange trip its been..."

David Massoni

Why Do I Need to Cover the Blender When Blending a Hot Liquid?

The laws of physics can be quite dangerous when you're not paying attention, like taking a sharp curve at high speed, falling down the stairs, or putting hot things in a blender. While we don't have to worry about any of those here, the last is courtesy of the Pressure-Temperature Law, which is sort of a composite of Boyle's law, Charles' law, and Gay-Lussac's law. All of these guys studied different facets of the same phenomenon—that gas expands when heated and contracts when cooled.

Have you ever bought balloons for your sweetheart on Valentine's Day, then walked outside into the snow and had all of the balloons deflate? You walk back into the store to demand a refund, and as you are waiting in line, the balloons magically begin to inflate again. Same thing.

When you put a hot liquid in the blender, the air above the liquid is heated. As it heats, it expands. As it expands, the pressure will build up. As the pressure builds up, the top of the blender will pop off, and the next thing you know, you're cleaning puree from the ceiling.

To prevent this, use a towel and your hand to cover the top of the blender. You can exert more pressure than that measly expanding gas.

Additionally, the center of the blender lid does more than allow you to add ingredients while blending. Used properly, it also lets steam (or gas) escape to avoid a buildup of pressure.

Don't make your Tang-Milk mixture in advance. Like all foods from the future, Tang's acidity levels will quickly curdle milk.

Tang-Creamsicle Shake

MAKES 2 THICK 8-OUNCE SHAKES

This shake was inspired by those Orange Julius kiosks in the shopping malls we hung out at when we were growing up, as well as by the orange Creamsicles we always had in our freezers. What is it about the combination of orange and cream? Orange alone can be overly acidic, but the addition of sweet vanilla ice cream tempers it down just so. We thought it would be fun to trash it up a notch by using neon-orange Tang powder for that high-in-the-sky taste.

¾ cup whole milk

1 tablespoon Tang orange drink powder

4 large scoops Vanilla Ice Cream (page 157) or Sweet Cream Ice Cream (page 147 or 156)

Add the milk and Tang to a blender, cover, and quickly pulse the blender to combine. Add the ice cream, cover, and blend (on "blend") until you see a whirlpool form—that's when you know it's done. Pour or spoon the shake into two tall glasses. Garnish with anything you'd like—Star Wars figurines, whipped cream, or a shake of more Tang powder. Serve with straws and spoons. Slam it!

NOTE: If using store-bought ice cream, avoid vanilla *bean.*

Date Shake

MAKES 2 THICK 8-OUNCE SHAKES

If you've never been to Southern California, you may be scratching
your head at this one. But if you have been there, then you know how
ubiquitous dates are, particularly in the desert communities east of Los
Angeles (where a significant amount of the date manufacturing in the
United States takes place). So if you ever find yourself driving out to Joshua
Tree National Park, you can find our favorite date shake at Windmill
Market & Produce. It's a little hole-in-the-wall market located just outside
Desert Hot Springs at the corner of Indian Avenue and Dillon Road. It's a
great way to beat the desert heat. We use almond milk. It pairs nicely with
the flavor of the dates and helps cut down on the sweetness.

1 cup pitted and
   chopped California
   or Medjool dates

1 cup almond milk

4 large scoops Vanilla
   Ice Cream (page 157)
   or Sweet Cream Ice
   Cream (page 147 or 156)

Add the dates and almond milk to a blender, cover, and puree
for 60 seconds, or until smooth. Add the ice cream, cover, and
blend on medium speed until you see a whirlpool form—that's
when you know it's done. Pour or spoon the shake into two tall
glasses. Garnish however you'd like—whipped cream, a drizzle
of honey, some psychotropics to help you discover your inner
spirit animal, or an old harmonica. Serve with shovels and a
hose. Or straws and spoons.

Salty Caramel Shake

MAKES 2 THICK 8-OUNCE SHAKES

Munchkins and lollipops. Finn and Jake. Salt and caramel. Some things are just meant to be together. We only have to look at our #1 cone, the Salty Pimp, to see how universal the love is for the combination of salt and caramel. So why not a sweet and salty shake? We suggest a plate of cookies to dunk into this one.

¾ cup whole milk

¼ cup Dulce de Leche (page 57)

1 teaspoon coarse sea salt

4 large scoops Vanilla Ice Cream (page 157) or Sweet Cream Ice Cream (page 147 or 156)

Add the milk, dulce de leche, and salt to a blender, cover, and quickly pulse the blender to combine. (The milk will taste very salty—don't fret.) Add the ice cream, cover, and blend (on "blend") until you see a whirlpool form—that's when you know it's done. Pour or spoon the shake into two tall glasses. Top with any garnish you'd like—cherries, whipped cream, some high-quality finishing salt, sea monkeys, whatever! Serve with straws and spoons. Enjoy!

JAM,
IF YOU'RE
FEELING
IT...

Chocolate–Peanut Butter Shake

MAKES 2 THICK 8-OUNCE SHAKES

The chocolate–peanut butter milk shake was the result of another suggestion from a customer. We always have peanut butter around for special requests, but we usually keep it off the menu because of allergy concerns. The customer asked Doug to make a chocolate shake with some added peanut butter. After getting the guy to state that he understood this was an experiment, and acknowledge that experiments sometimes fail, and that if this happened, it would not be bitched about on Yelp, Doug went to the shake machine and whipped up a really delicious artery-clogger.

¾ cup whole milk

1 tablespoon chocolate syrup (or a big squirt if using a squeeze bottle)

4 large scoops Chocolate Ice Cream (page 149)

¼ cup smooth peanut butter

Add the milk and chocolate syrup to a blender, cover, and quickly pulse the blender to combine. Add the ice cream and peanut butter, cover, and blend (on "blend") until you see a whirlpool form—that's when you know it's done. Pour or spoon the shake into two tall glasses. Top with any garnish you'd like—cherries, whipped cream, shaved chocolate, Lipitor, whatever you damned well please. It's your party. Own it! Serve with straws and spoons.

Maple-Biscoff Shake

MAKES 2 THICK 8-OUNCE SHAKES

It's cold and snowy outside. Your tan is gone, and you can't justify going outside in flip-flops anymore. All your parents care about is what colleges you're going to apply to and that damn SAT. All you want to do is get into Eastern Bloc with your fake ID. Like they would know the difference. So, how do you compromise? Invite the Beckys over, raid your dad's drink cart, and blend up some of these boozy babies!

¾ cup whole milk

2 tablespoons maple syrup

¼ cup smooth Biscoff spread—aka speculoos

4 large scoops Vanilla Ice Cream (page 157) or Sweet Cream Ice Cream (page 147 or 156)

Add the milk, maple syrup, and Biscoff spread to a blender, cover, and puree the mixture, about 30 seconds. Add the ice cream, cover, and blend (this time on "blend") until you see a whirlpool form—that's when you know it's done. Pour or spoon the shake into two tall glasses. Top with any garnish you'd like—cherries, whipped cream, a drizzle more of maple syrup, Styrofoam packing chips, or something even more delicious. Serve with straws and spoons.

BOOZY VERSION: Want to booze up this sucker? Reduce the amount of milk to ½ cup and add ¼ cup bourbon.

Hey Big Gays —
What can I say?
Have a cool summer
+ eat ICE CREAM!
Love, JANE
The Go-Go's

Coffee Shake

MAKES 2 THICK 8-OUNCE SHAKES

This shake uses the same homemade coffee concentrate as our Coffee Ice Cream (page 152). It's an easy way to make a robust shake that's not too sweet but high on a strong, rich coffee taste. Between the caffeine and sugar, we hope it imparts a bit of a buzz—but with your tolerance levels, it seems unlikely. Tweaker!

4 large scoops Vanilla Ice Cream (page 157) or Sweet Cream Ice Cream (page 147 or 156)

¾ cup Coffee Base (page 153)

Add the ice cream and coffee base to a blender, cover, and blend (on medium or "blend" if the machine has that option) until you see a whirlpool form—that's when you know it's done. Pour or spoon the shake into two tall glasses. Top with any garnish you find enticing—whipped cream, cacao nibs, a drizzle of flavored syrup or liqueur, chopped chocolate-covered espresso beans, or five live salamanders. Anything goes! Serve with straws and spoons.

NOTE: For a mocha shake, just substitute Chocolate Ice Cream (page 149) for the vanilla.

Ice Cream Social Playlist

60 UR

UR POSITION IEC TYPE I • NORMAL

FAIRY PRINCESS

Princess MuPaul

A

Hannah Montana
"Ice Cream Freeze
(Let's Chill)"

X
"Los Angeles"

Van Halen
"Ice Cream Man"

Little Eva
"The Loco-Motion"

The B-52's
"Private Idaho"

The Rolling Stones
"Mother's Little Helper"

Beck
"Sexx Laws"

John Mellencamp
"Jack and Diane"

Jan and Dean
"Popsicle"

B

The Ramones
"Blitzkrieg Bop"

Mötley Crüe
"Kickstart My Heart"

The Magnetic Fields
"The Luckiest Guy on the
Lower East Side"

Odyssey
"Native New Yorker"

Iggy Pop
"Lust for Life"

Brady Bunch
"Candy (Sugar Shoppe)"

DJ Cutlet
"Big Gay Ice Cream Truck"

Jane Wiedlin
"Big Gay Ice Cream Song"

The Choinkwich

MAKES 4 CHOINKWICHES

Early in our test-kitchen experiments, months before the truck manifested itself, we started screwing around with bacon and chocolate ice cream. The chocolatier Vosges makes a chocolate bar with smoky bacon in it, and we'd been fans of it for a while, so that was definitely an inspiration for us. We fried up some bacon, pulled it into bits, and topped some chocolate ice cream with it. The initial taste was terrific, but the ice cream quickly melted in our mouths, leaving us chewing cold, gummy bacon. Then, when Doug watched someone eat an ice cream sandwich, he had an epiphany. You've got to bite *through* the cookie, so adding a bacon layer seemed like a no-brainer! Bryan caramelized countless batches of bacon, and there we were.

At first we just called it "that bacon ice cream sandwich thing." Doug turned to our Twitter following for suggestions, and numerous ideas were shot down before we chose Choinkwich. Chocolate, OINK (for the bacon, but we think you probably guessed that), and WICH for sandwich. Actually, the winning name was suggested by Doug, but we've never divulged that until now.

When we opened our first shop, we teamed up with two companies to help us put the Choinkwich on our menu full time. The Treats Truck made great chocolate cookies for us and Bacon Marmalade made a great bacon spread for us. When Bacon Marmalade closed up shop, though, we retired the Choinkwich from active duty. So, until it returns, we're giving you everything you need to know to whip up your own.

8 Chocolate Cookies (page 124) or store-bought chocolate cookies

4 scoops Chocolate Ice Cream (page 149)

4 pieces Caramelized Bacon (recipe follows)

Place 4 of the cookies upside down on a cookie sheet. Place a scoop of ice cream on each cookie. Fold or tear the bacon slices and place one atop each scoop. Finish by gently pressing a second cookie over each sandwich. Eat immediately!

NOTE: **You can wrap each Choinkwich in wax paper, deli-sandwich-style, and keep in the freezer if necessary, but we prefer the flavor and texture of caramelized bacon that hasn't been frozen.**

WORK FAST SO THE ICE CREAM DOESN'T MELT TOO MUCH!

PICKIEST EATER

When I met Doug and Bryan, Big Gay Ice Cream was brand-new and no one could tell a Bea Arthur from a Salty Pimp. This was a long time ago. Doug had long wavy blond hair, and life back then was so carefree. Anyway, I walked past the truck one day, grabbed a Choinkwich, and felt my knees start to tremble. I wrote about them in a column I was doing for Delta's <u>Sky Magazine,</u> and their business went through the roof.

Now they don't take my calls, and they ignore me when I buzz up looking for a place to crash in New York. Bryan has a court order requiring me to stay at least one hundred yards away from the truck. Fuck that, they are so selfish. I am opening a Big Straight Wiener truck in Minneapolis next year. I am sure I will hear from their lawyer. Doug is a good kisser. Bryan has busier hands when he cuddles. They are blowing up and don't have time for the little people. Sad.

Andrew Zimmer

Andrew Zimmern

Caramelized Bacon

MAKES 9 TO 12 PIECES

EQUIPMENT

Rimmed baking sheet
and a wire cooling
rack

Loaf pan

Tongs

Another cooling rack
or a nonstick baking
sheet

Pot holders or oven
mitts

A steady hand

Open kitchen window

A jar to collect the
molten sugar-grease
mixture

Scouring pads

Burn cream

Telephone number for
a rug-and-furniture
cleaning service

INGREDIENTS

2 cups turbinado sugar

Half a 16-ounce
package thick-cut
bacon

When we were making the Choinkwich 1.0 on the truck, we tried different types of sweeteners. The easiest choice turned out the best results: bags of Dominican Republican brown sugar from the bodega across from our apartment. Turbinado (aka Sugar in the Raw) sugar is more available and when we were perfecting the recipe it was the closest thing to what we were looking for, replicating that deep brown sugar flavor and large crystals of our "bodega sugar."

Caramelizing bacon is like trying to make a grilled steak on your stovetop: there will be smoke. Also, everything you own will smell like bacon after you are done. This may or may not be a good thing. Be sure to temporarily disconnect your smoke detector.

Arrange an oven rack in the center of the oven. Preheat the oven to 375°F.

Set the wire rack on the baking sheet. Pour one-third of the sugar into the loaf pan. One at a time, place the slices of bacon in the pan and press into the sugar to coat, then flip and coat the other side of the slices and lay on the wire rack; space the slices about ½ inch apart. (Note: Work fast! The bacon is easiest to handle when it's cold.) Discard the remaining sugar.

Bake for 10 minutes, then gingerly remove the baking sheet from the oven. (CAREFUL! The bottom of the pan will be full of molten sugar and bacon grease—a powerful burn-worthy combination!) Flip each slice of bacon with tongs. Put the baking sheet back in the oven and bake for another 5 to 7 minutes, until the bacon is a dark golden color but not burnt. Remove the baking sheet from the oven—MIND THE GREASE. Use your tongs to transfer each slice to another cooling rack or nonstick baking sheet to cool. Don't worry if the bacon isn't crispy—it will harden as it cools. For best results, use immediately.

Chocolate Cookies

MAKES ABOUT 40 COOKIES

This recipe is for a basic but very tasty chocolate cookie. "Not too fancy, always delicious"—that's the way Kim Ima, owner of the Treats Truck and author of this recipe, approaches baking. When we decided to start making our own ice cream sandwiches, the only chocolate cookies we could imagine using were the ones that Kim used for her sandwich cookies. (Excerpted from *The Treats Truck Baking Book* by Kim Ima, HarperCollins, 2011.)

2 cups all-purpose flour

1 cup plus 1 tablespoon unsweetened cocoa powder

1¾ cups sugar

⅜ teaspoon baking soda

½ teaspoon salt

½ pound (2 sticks) plus 2 tablespoons unsalted butter, cut into cubes and softened

5 tablespoons whole milk

1½ teaspoons pure vanilla extract

Preheat the oven to 350°F and grease a baking sheet or line it with parchment paper. In a large bowl or mixer, combine the flour, cocoa powder, sugar, baking soda, and salt. Add the butter and mix until a dough forms. Add the milk and vanilla and mix until the dough is smooth. Mold the dough into 1 big block, wrap it in plastic wrap or put it in a container, and refrigerate it for at least 30 minutes to overnight. Roll out the dough to about ¼ inch thick. Cut out the cookies with a round cookie cutter (or any shape you like) and place at least 1 inch apart on the baking sheet. Bake for 8 to 10 minutes. If the cookies look a little soft when you take them out, don't worry! They'll firm up as they cool. Cool in the pan or move after a few minutes to a wire rack.

Store in an airtight container.

SCIENCE CLUB

What's the Difference Between All These Sugars?

Most people are familiar with white (granulated) sugar and powdered (confectioners') sugar, but there are lots of other ways to sweeten your ice cream.

Granulated sugar is usually made from sugarcane and is highly processed to remove the natural brown color. Removing the natural brown color also changes the taste and texture (see below). The chemical that makes up common sugar is *sucrose*. Sucrose is a disaccharide, because it is composed of two sugar subunits and is digested as glucose and fructose.

Powdered sugar is white sugar that has been milled to a finer grain and has cornstarch added to prevent clumping.

Molasses is usually made from sugarcane juice that has been boiled and had most of the sugar (in the form of sucrose) removed. It's somewhat sweet, but it is usually used more for its rich flavor rather than for sweetness.

Brown sugar is refined white sugar that has had molasses added to it. The amount of molasses (usually between 3% and 10%) determines whether it is "light brown" or "dark brown." Adding molasses to white sugar means the color and taste can be tightly controlled.

Turbinado, demerara, and muscovado sugars (also called raw sugars) are made from sugarcane, but are less refined than white and brown sugars. Muscovado is the darkest of these sugars and has the most residual minerals, but the mineral content is quite negligible, so there aren't really health benefits to using it.

Corn syrup, as its name implies, is made from corn. Because it is a liquid instead of a solid, it can often produce smoother ice cream because it won't crystallize.

Light corn syrup and *dark corn syrup* can usually be used interchangeably. Light corn syrup has a more delicate flavor and a slight vanilla taste, while dark corn syrup has a touch of molasses flavor and is better for baked goods.

High-fructose corn syrup is different from the corn syrup you buy at the grocery store because it is chemically modified to convert glucose to fructose, tastes sweeter on the tongue, and bypasses part of the digestive process, triggering the creation of fats and insulin. It is used in highly processed foods.

Agave nectar is made from the agave plant, which is also used for making tequila. It has been touted as a more healthful alternative to sugar or corn syrup, but in reality it is not healthy at all. Although it won't give you the blood-sugar spike that regular sugar does (thus the "low-glycemic" claim), the high fructose content can cause other problems because it is processed in the liver into fat deposits. Agave nectar is a highly processed sweetener and contains even more fructose than high-fructose corn syrup.

Honey and *maple syrup* are the most "natural" sweeteners because they are simply harvested and bottled with minimal changes. Make sure you get a natural maple syrup without additives.

If you must avoid sugars altogether there are numerous substitutes. Most of them contain a mélange of chemicals, so long-term usage may cause more problems than just using white sugar. If you must use something other than what's listed above, consider *Stevia*. It's made from a natural herb and contains no actual sugar molecules. The Stevia you can buy off the shelf is highly processed but it's still better for you than aspartame, sucralose, or xylitol.

Senior Year

LET'S GO ALL THE WAY!
SORBETS AND ICE CREAMS

SHOP CLASS

And We Thought Starting a Truck Was Hard!

The Leap

During our third year with the truck, we realized we needed to decide whether we were in the ice cream business or we weren't. Doug was still performing and working toward his doctoral degree, and Bryan was going to his office every day. If we were going to move forward, we had to commit fully—so we took a deep breath, quit our old lives, and jumped right in.

We also realized that the future of Big Gay Ice Cream was not all about the truck. There was no way in hell we wanted to have a fleet of trucks, but opening a store made sense to us. It seemed part of our natural—if somewhat unexpected— evolution. Hey, This Shit's for Real Now!

We knew all along that East 7th Street, in the East Village, would be perfect for us. The block of East 7th Street between First Avenue and Avenue A has been written about on numerous occasions as one of the great dining destinations in the city. We'd go there and eat at Porchetta, Sara Jenkins' fabulous roast pork shop; a great Greek restaurant called Pylos; Caracas Arepa Bar (when there wasn't a line); and Luke's Lobster. At a chance meeting, our friend Luke Holden, now a lobster mogul, informed us that a juice bar on his block was closing that very day. Within a few weeks, we had taken over their lease.

We knew opening our first shop would be a big deal. It was important to us to control every aspect of it, including when we announced its opening. To the outside world it was business as usual with the truck. But behind an anonymous storefront with newspapers in the windows announcing Osama bin Laden's death, we were frantically remodeling. Our desire for secrecy soon reached borderline paranoia, to the point that when Bryan saw a tweet from an editor from the website Eater saying he was at a bar nearby, we actually shut down our renovations for the day and left the neighborhood.

You Know What This Place Needs? 6,000 Swarovski Crystals!

Designing our shop was the first opportunity for us to have people walk into our idea of a space that was Big and Gay. Well, not Big. The shop itself would end up being very small. But certainly Gay. Somehow Doug had the idea of putting a giant minotaur with Bea Arthur's head on the wall. Ultimately, that proved too ambitious, so we settled on a mural of a life-size unicorn.

Sam Simon, a muralist we found via Twitter, usually painted nurseries and children's rooms, creating fantastical landscapes, so we figured he could handle a unicorn.

Swarovski crystals were always part of our plan with Sam—we budgeted for 1,000 of them—but by the end there were in excess of 6,000. Sam and his assistant used a pencil to dab a little dot of glue on the wall and then apply a crystal. For three days this was repeated over and over again, more than 6,000 times. It was both hypnotic and disturbing to watch.

Father Guido Bourdain

We opened the store in 2011 on Labor Day weekend, quite possibly the busiest holiday weekend of the year. It was a decision that, in retrospect, was more than a little psychotic. We'd only had about two days for the staff to come in to practice their cone-making skills for their friends, our neighbors on the block, and random passersby. We'd overlooked a few critical points, like expediting. And line management. And breaks. And our sanity. That

THAT'S STEPHIN MERRITT OF THE MAGNETIC FIELDS PERFORMING IN OUR SHOP!

first day we worked nonstop from 7 a.m. until 3 a.m. It wasn't until day two that we even thought to take customer names to keep the orders straight. But by the time we opened our door for the first time, people had been lining up for over an hour.

We had a lovingly tragic drag queen, Ari Kiki the Hot Mess, giving out "free babies" and entertaining waiting customers. We had roller derby girls passing out Big Gay flyers, and a contrabassoon octet called Contraband. Contrabassoons are twice as big and twice as low as regular bassoons, and it's rare to see even two of them in the same place. Doug's friend Harry managed to assemble a whole group, and Doug conducted them as they played the opening of *Also sprach Zarathustra*, the 1896 tone poem by Richard Strauss that is more well known as the music from *2001: A Space Odyssey*. There was also a keyboardist (DJ Cutlet, who had written our very first theme song two years prior) on hand to bang out the timpani part.

We had an opening benediction given by Anthony Bourdain, who was wearing a priest's outfit we'd bought at a neighborhood Halloween shop. Then, after all the pomp and circumstance, business started a few minutes later. We had no idea what the hell we were doing.

But it was a great day. Eventually we established a good workflow, with Doug making cones and Bryan working as the expediter, overseeing him and the rest of the staff. At some point, TV personality Stacy London showed up and got people talking and tweeting, and Marco Canora, the chef and owner of the acclaimed Hearth restaurant, stopped by to lend his support and get ice cream for his daughter. We went nonstop from noon until after midnight—the line was ninety minutes long all day—and on top of making a bazillion cones, we spent two hours cleaning up after it was all over. We were back the next morning at around eight o'clock to make adjustments and do it all over again.

Social Studies 101

CUSTOMERS WHO REALLY SHOULDN'T DECIDE THEIR OWN ICE CREAM ORDERS

1. Junkies

I had to research why they all want something really sugary, and it turns out that long-term heroin use somehow causes hypoglycemia. If a customer staggers up and I see they've got teeny little pupils, I take the lead. They are too incoherent to figure out what to order, so I throw out the two sweetest options: butterscotch sauce or cherry dip. I've never been wrong.

2. Stoners

When our truck parked in the East Village on a weekend night, small groups would come up giggling. They would touch the menu and say, "Oh, that one is SO pretty!" I would tell them to order a vanilla cone covered in Trix cereal, and then I would invariably hear something like, "Oh my god, it's SO pretty!" Never fails.

3. First-Timers

Otherwise known as the "I don't know what I want so you figure it out for me" customer. Salty Pimp. No need for any other options.

4. Tweakers

Why do people do crystal meth? Gross. Occasionally a customer would come to the truck with pupils the size of quarters, sweating through his or her clothes. Too screwed up to communicate. I figured their throats hurt too much from the drugs, so I would suggest a cup (not a cone) of vanilla or a vanilla shake. No toppings. Bingo. Also, we dealt with their money up front. Their hands were usually too shaky and their brains too addled to make change. Drugs are bad. Don't do drugs.

5. Little Kids

Parents sometimes overload their children's brains with options. "Honey, you like Nutella, maybe you'd like that in your cone? Chocolate or rainbow sprinkles? Do you want a twist, you know, vanilla and chocolate twisted together? Cherry dip? That's the red dip."

One time a dad was suggesting all sorts of options and his overwhelmed child whizzed himself. Another little girl lifted up her dress over her head—it was all just too much for her. Trust me, what that kid wants is a vanilla cone with rainbow sprinkles.

Bonus: Chain Smokers

If someone lit their cigarette with another cigarette while looking at our menu, I offered cayenne pepper as a topping. They obviously decimated their own taste buds, so I hit 'em with something strong. Nothing else made an impression.

SORBETS & ICE CREAMS

Here we go, folks. It's time to start putting your ice cream machine to work. There are plenty of great treats in your grocery store's freezer section, but few of them hold a candle to what you can do at home. You could make a vaguely rational argument that you're scared of most every appliance, but it's not going to work here. Unless you have a chest freezer that you could fall into (that's the way most everyone on the early 1990s show <u>Picket Fences</u> died), you have no excuse for not trying these recipes.

These recipes are all pretty simple, so the quality of ingredients is key. You want great dairy—spend the extra money, it will shine through. Get high-quality sugar. And if you've got a friend with chickens, get really screwed up, then sneak over there before dawn and steal some eggs from them. It'll be a fun adventure for you, your ice cream will rock, and your friends will have an awesome story about seeing you naked out by the chicken house.

Concord Grape Sorbet MAKES 1 QUART

We're both suckers (pun intended) for grape ice pops: we keep Edy's Grape Fruit Bars in constant rotation in our freezer. So a grape sorbet recipe came naturally to us. We decided to keep it simple, but we wanted it to taste like getting hit across the face with a bunch of grapes. Fresh Concord grapes can be hard to find—they are mainly grown to be turned into juice—so stick with the juice. Make sure it's not mixed with other juices or any sweeteners.

2 cups Concord grape juice (100% pure, no sugar added)

1 cup Simple Syrup (page 141)

1 tablespoon saba

Combine the grape juice, simple syrup, and saba in a medium bowl and stir to mix. Transfer the mixture to a 1-quart container, cover, and refrigerate for at least 4 hours, until completely cold.

Freeze the sorbet mixture in an ice cream maker according to the manufacturer's instructions. When it is finished, transfer the sorbet to an airtight container and freeze for at least 2 hours to harden. The sorbet can be stored in the freezer for up to 5 days.

A NOTE ABOUT ICE CREAM MACHINES

We tested these recipes in two home machines and recommend both. The Cuisinart ICE-30BC Pure Indulgence 2-Quart Automatic Ice Cream Maker (the stainless steel version) requires you to keep its inner drum in your freezer until used. It's a great relatively inexpensive machine, easy to use, and easy to clean. For those willing to invest in something bigger and badder and who have the shelf space, there's the Breville BCI600XL Smart Scoop Ice Cream Maker. This has a built-in compressor that drops its core temperature, so it doesn't have components that need to be kept in the freezer. It's not cheap, but it's certainly the top dog in its category. It's quieter by far than any other ice cream maker we've ever used. Except, that is, when it plays "Turkey in the Straw" to let you know your ice cream is ready, just like your neighborhood ice cream truck.

Stay cool this summer.
See you next year!
Love, David

Mountain Dew Sorbet

MAKES 1 QUART

We were having lunch one day at a well-known Brooklyn restaurant where a friend was the pastry chef. (She and the restaurant shall remain nameless.) She brought out a secret ice cream flavor she was working on for a special event: Tetrahydrocannabinol. THC. Pot ice cream. It tasted exactly like you'd think it would, and it got us thinking about the idea of Stoner Ice Cream. This sorbet lies snugly between stoner ice cream and "This thing needs some tequila!" The choice is yours.

2½ cups Mountain Dew (one 20-ounce bottle)

1½ cups Simple Syrup (page 141)

1 teaspoon fresh lemon juice

1 teaspoon fresh lime juice

Bring the Mountain Dew to a boil in a medium saucepan over medium heat. Reduce the heat and simmer for about 45 minutes, until the soda has reduced to 1½ cups.

Transfer the Mountain Dew to a 1-quart container, add the simple syrup, and stir to incorporate. Cover and refrigerate for at least 4 hours, until completely cold.

Add the lemon juice and lime juice to the sorbet mixture and freeze in an ice cream maker according to the manufacturer's instructions. When it is finished, transfer the sorbet to an airtight container and freeze for at least 2 hours to harden. The sorbet can be stored in the freezer for up to 5 days.

Pear & Ginger Sorbet

MAKES 1 QUART

Making infused simple syrups is extremely, well, simple! You need only simmer your desired flavor (in this case, ginger, but it could be virtually any fruit, herb, or candy) in water and sugar. Here, the ginger adds a seasonal sweet-heat bite to the pear flavor. Once you make this recipe, you'll begin imagining how to transfer the "infused simple syrup + fruit juice" formula to your own combinations.

1 cup sugar

A 2-inch piece of fresh ginger, peeled and chopped into ½-inch cubes

1 cup water

2 cups pear juice (no sugar added)

½ teaspoon fresh lemon juice

Combine the sugar, ginger, and water in a small saucepan and steep over low heat for 1 hour, stirring occasionally.

Add the pear juice and lemon juice, stir, and keep over low heat for another 15 minutes. Strain the syrup into a 1-quart container; discard the ginger. Cover and refrigerate for at least 4 hours, until completely cold.

Freeze the sorbet mixture in an ice cream maker according to the manufacturer's instructions. When it is finished, transfer the sorbet to an airtight container and freeze for at least 2 hours to harden. The sorbet can be stored in the freezer for up to 5 days.

Peppercoke Sorbet
MAKES 1 QUART

Soda sorbets are a lot of fun to make. Think of quaint mini versions of science project volcanoes as their carbonation simmers away. We always have Mexican Coca-Cola around our shops for coke floats. The Coke we buy really is imported from Mexico, and there are two things about it that are awesome: it contains cane sugar, not corn syrup, and it comes in glass bottles. Coca-Cola has a mild peppery component, which we decided to ramp up exponentially for this recipe.

2½ cups Coca-Cola (preferably Mexican Coca-Cola)

1 heaping tablespoon whole black peppercorns

1 heaping tablespoon whole pink peppercorns

1½ cups Simple Syrup (recipe follows)

Combine the Coca-Cola and black and pink peppercorns in a medium saucepan and bring to a boil over medium heat. Reduce the heat and simmer for about 45 minutes, until the soda has reduced to 1½ cups.

Strain the syrup into a 1-quart container; discard the peppercorns. Add the simple syrup and stir to incorporate. Cover and refrigerate for at least 4 hours, until completely cold.

Freeze the sorbet mixture in an ice cream maker according to the manufacturer's instructions. When it is finished, transfer the sorbet to an airtight container and freeze for at least 2 hours to harden. The sorbet can be stored in the freezer for up to 5 days.

Simple Syrup
MAKES 5 CUPS

A basic simple syrup is equal parts sugar and water. If you don't need as much as this recipe makes, just cut it down.

4 cups sugar

4 cups hot water

Combine the sugar and hot water in a large saucepan or heatproof bowl and stir until the sugar is completely dissolved. Transfer to a covered container and refrigerate. The syrup can be kept refrigerated for weeks.

Cranberry & White Chocolate Sorbet

MAKES 1 QUART

YEAH DUDE! See you at the Beach.... John Booth

Cranberries pop when you simmer them. Pretend they're screaming in agony as you boil them alive! You can use fresh or frozen cranberries; chances are you won't find them fresh except around the holidays. This sorbet isn't terribly sweet, which is one reason why the addition of chunks of white chocolate works so well. You can rag on white chocolate all you want—we know, we know, it's not really chocolate. Blah blah blah. It works great here, so stop your bitchin' and get cookin' (and then freezin').

2 cups (8 ounces) fresh or frozen cranberries

2 cups water

½ cup orange juice

¾ cup sugar

Juice of ½ lemon

2 tablespoons Grand Marnier (optional)

2 ounces white chocolate, roughly chopped

Combine the cranberries, water, and orange juice in a large saucepan and bring to a simmer over medium heat. After a few minutes, the berries will begin to pop and lose their color into the water. Stir frequently and smash the berries up a bit as you do. After 15 minutes of simmering, add the sugar and stir until it has fully dissolved, about another 2 minutes, then remove from the heat.

Add the lemon juice and Grand Marnier, if using. Allow to cool in the saucepan for 15 minutes, then strain the syrup into a 1-quart container; discard the berry skins. Cover and refrigerate for at least 4 hours, until completely cold.

Freeze the sorbet mixture in an ice cream maker according to the manufacturer's instructions. At the mix-in stage of the freezing process, following the manufacturer's instructions, add the white chocolate. When it is finished, transfer the sorbet to an airtight container and freeze for at least 2 hours to harden. The sorbet can be stored in the freezer for up to 5 days.

Cheater Soft-Serve Ice Cream MAKES 1 QUART

During our first summer, a writer contacted us for an interview. His name sounded sort of freaky, so we looked him up and it turned out he was John T. Edge, a James Beard Foundation award winner and writer for the *New York Times*. What the hell did he want with us? Well, he wanted to feature us in a new book about food trucks. Since that first interview, we've become good friends with Mr. Edge. Here is a very clever recipe from that book to put our toppings on. (Excerpted from *The Truck Food Cookbook* by John T. Edge, Workman Publishing, 2012.)

3 cups store-bought vanilla ice cream, slightly softened

1 cup Whipped Cream (page 88)

2 to 4 tablespoons Awesomesauce (page 59) or store-bought chocolate syrup (optional)

Scoop the ice cream into the bowl of an electric stand mixer. Add the whipped cream and, if using, the Awesomesauce or chocolate syrup, and beat until thoroughly blended. Cover the ice cream tightly, either by placing it in a container with a lid or by wrapping the bowl several times in plastic wrap. Place the ice cream in the freezer for at least 12 hours. Believe it or not, it will still be slightly soft after that time. Then, it's ready to eat, with or without your choice of toppings.

PROBABLY NOT THE FIRST TIME TRIX CAME TO THE JAMES BEARD HOUSE ...

THE JAMES BEARD HOUSE

PLAQUE DONATED BY
THE NEW YORK ASSOCIATION OF COOKING TEAC

Sweet Cream Ice Cream (Philly-Style)

MAKES 1 QUART

Ice creams made without eggs or other emulsifiers, often called "Philadelphia style," are quicker and easier to make than custard-based ice creams. Ideally, they should be consumed soon after they are made. How Philly-style ice creams will hold up in your freezer depends on a number of factors, including how airtight the containers are and how much fat is in the ice cream. But really, just eat these ice creams right away. No one's looking. By the way, that shirt you're wearing is fabulous.

1½ cups whole milk

1½ cups heavy cream

⅔ cup sugar

1 teaspoon kosher salt

Warm the milk and cream in a small saucepan over medium heat, stirring frequently, until the mixture begins to steam. Add the sugar and salt and stir until completely dissolved. Remove from the heat, and transfer the ice cream base to a 1-quart container. Let cool, then cover and refrigerate for at least 6 hours, until completely cold.

Freeze the mixture in an ice cream maker according to the manufacturer's instructions. When it is finished, start eating or transfer the ice cream to an airtight container and freeze for up to 2 hours to harden (but not longer), and then eat.

TRIX ICE CREAM: Before freezing the ice cream, place a medium bowl in the freezer. When the ice cream is ready, transfer it to the bowl and fold in 1 cup Trix cereal. Then scoop the Trix ice cream into a 1-quart container and freeze for at least 2 hours to harden.

SCIENCE CLUB

What Is Homogenization, and Why Should I Care?

Have you ever seen fresh raw milk, where the cream separates into a thick layer at the top? It's almost like butter. You can spoon it into your coffee like cream or shake up the bottle to reincorporate it into the milk. If you remove it, the remaining milk is actually pretty low in fat.

Modern milk manufacturers decided that consumers didn't like that plug at the top. It looked too much like spoiled milk. So homogenization was born. When milk is *homogenized,* the fat particles are broken into very small particles that stay in the milk and don't rise to the top. Homogenization also allows large milk manufacturers (who combine milk from several different dairies and types of cow) to make a more uniform and consistent final product—ultimately so they can control the final taste and fat content.

So why does homogenization matter? Well, there are a lot of people who think they are lactose intolerant when they really are just drinking the wrong kind of milk. When the fat particles are mechanically broken into smaller particles, they can pass too quickly through the digestive process and not be digested. Proteins that *should* be digested are allowed to pass into the bloodstream. This can cause a host of belly problems that we won't get into in a cookbook. Suffice to say, every time you eat processed food—homogenized milk included—you are ingesting something your body was not designed to digest.

Now, don't confuse this with *pasteurization.* This is a process where milk is heated in order to kill bacteria and is usually required for any milk sold commercially. Pasteurized milk also has a longer shelf life.

So: *homogenization* = bad, *pasteurization* = good.

One other note: Different types of cows produce different kinds of milk. Jersey cows (the brown ones) have a much higher "solids content" than Holstein cows (the black-and-white ones). This means that Jersey milk is much richer, and that will affect the taste and texture of everything you make with the milk, from ice cream to yogurt or cheese to your morning cappuccino. Ronnybrook Farm Dairy in New York's Hudson Valley—who provide us with our East Coast dairy—produces a line of nonhomogenized milk called Creamline. If you can find nonhomogenized Jersey milk near you, thank us later, after you've had a mouthful of that deliciousness!

Chocolate Ice Cream

MAKES 1 QUART

People don't *want* chocolate. People *need* chocolate. The first few ice cream trucks we used were so beat up that on a hot day their generators didn't put out enough power to freeze two kinds of ice cream. To keep the vanilla flowing, we'd have to turn off chocolate, and man, people would flip the hell out! That's when we learned that we'd better show chocolate some respect. Here's a chocolate ice cream recipe that we really love, along with a few easy variations.

1¼ cups whole milk

1¼ cups heavy cream

½ cup sugar

2 ounces dark chocolate

2 tablespoons unsweetened cocoa powder

½ teaspoon kosher salt

½ teaspoon Grand Marnier (optional)

Warm the milk and cream in a medium saucepan over medium heat, stirring frequently, until the mixture begins to steam. Add the sugar and stir until completely dissolved.

Meanwhile, warm the chocolate in a microwave for about 30 seconds to melt it. Add the chocolate to the saucepan and stir for about 3 minutes, until thoroughly combined. Whisk in the cocoa powder and salt until dissolved. Then reduce the heat and cook at a low temperature, stirring, for 2 to 3 minutes. Remove from the heat and stir in the Grand Marnier, if using.

Transfer the mixture to a 1-quart container, cover, and refrigerate for at least 6 hours. The chilled mixture will be quite thick, so give it a good whisk before pouring it into your ice cream maker. Freeze according to the manufacturer's instructions and eat immediately.

SPICY CHOCOLATE: Add ¼ teaspoon (or ½ teaspoon for extra spicy) cayenne pepper and 1 cinnamon stick when you add the melted chocolate. Remove the cinnamon stick before chilling.

SMOKY CHOCOLATE: Add ½ teaspoon chipotle chili powder and 1 cinnamon stick when you add the melted chocolate. Remove the cinnamon stick before chilling.

SALTY CHOCOLATE: Add 2 teaspoons high-quality flaky sea salt or fleur de sel in a slow pour during the mix-in stage of your ice cream maker.

Hi Ice Cream Boys...
"Sweetest" You Guys Have The Ice Box!
♡ MINDY

Strawberry Ice Cream

MAKES 1 QUART

Making ice cream that contains berries is a bit of a trick to do properly, as berries are mostly water and that will contribute to an overly icy final product. To prevent this, finely chop the berries, sugar them, and allow them to macerate overnight. You'll draw out a good percentage of the moisture, and sugaring them will boost their flavor. Minimum ice, maximum taste.

1½ cups finely chopped ripe, in-season strawberries or finely chopped thawed frozen strawberries

½ teaspoon pure vanilla extract

½ cup sugar

Base for Sweet Cream Ice Cream (page 147 or 156), thoroughly chilled

Place the strawberries, vanilla, and sugar in a bowl or sealable container and mix well. Cover and refrigerate overnight.

Set a strainer over a large bowl (or use a colander) and pour in the berry mixture. Let the mixture drain for 15 minutes, stirring every few minutes to release more of the liquid. Transfer the strawberries to a clean container and place in the refrigerator. Save the strawberry liquid for another purpose, if desired (we like to add it to milk and chug it).

Freeze the sweet cream base in an ice cream maker according to the manufacturer's instructions. Remove the strawberries from the refrigerator. At the mix-in stage of the freezing process, following the manufacturer's instructions, add the strawberries. When the ice cream is finished, take a bite. If you don't eat it all then and there, transfer to an airtight container and freeze for up to 2 hours.

NOTE: Adding ⅓ cup of this strawberry mixture to our Vanilla Shake (page 107) makes a most righteous strawberry shake.

Guys,
Have a "Cool" Summer!
So much fun at the Prom.
You rock

Love,
Jen

Coffee Ice Cream

MAKES 1 QUART

Doug likes a strong cup of coffee with some whole milk and no sugar, and you'll probably realize that if you make the recipe as written. If you like a less potent brew, just cut back on the amount of coffee and reduce the steeping time a bit. You can also add more sugar to taste. If you like flavored syrups in your coffee, drizzle your favorites over the finished ice cream before serving.

1¼ cups Coffee Base (recipe follows)

1¼ cups heavy cream

⅓ cup sugar

½ teaspoon pure vanilla extract

¼ teaspoon kosher salt

Warm the coffee base and cream in a medium saucepan over medium heat, stirring frequently, for about 5 minutes, until the mixture begins to steam. Add the sugar and stir for about 3 minutes, until completely dissolved. Stir in the vanilla and salt and continue to cook for another 2 minutes, whisking frequently.

Remove from the heat and transfer the mixture to a 1-quart container. Cover and refrigerate for at least 6 hours.

Thoroughly whisk the mixture, then freeze in an ice cream maker according to the manufacturer's instructions. Eat immediately.

VARIATION: Chopped chocolate-covered espresso beans make a great mix-in. Use about ½ cup and add them during the mix-in phase.

Hi Boys,
Ice Cream is
Better Than An
O.T.P.H.J.

Coffee Base

MAKES 1 QUART

Our coffee ice cream and milk shakes use the same "flavor base." It's easy as hell to make. Use your French press, follow these instructions, and you'll have enough coffee flavor base for a batch of Coffee Ice Cream and a Coffee Shake (page 118) or three.

1 quart whole milk

2 ounces freshly ground coffee beans (our favorite, of course, is our own Big Gay Blend)

Heat the milk in a medium saucepan over medium heat, stirring frequently to avoid scorching, until it is steaming and starting to simmer.

Place the coffee in an 8-cup French press, then carefully add the steaming milk. (If you have a smaller French press, simply do multiple batches.) Stir thoroughly, then place the top on the press and let the mixture steep for 20 minutes, opening the press once or twice to stir the coffee again.

Press out the grounds according to the manufacturer's instructions. Pour the mixture into an airtight container and refrigerate until completely cold before using. The base can be refrigerated for up to 1 week.

Extra-Virgin Olive Oil Ice Cream

MAKES 1 QUART

Olive oil has been in our ice cream topping repertoire from the first "test kitchen" that we held to experiment with what to offer on the truck. Meredith Kurtzman makes a positively ferocious olive oil gelato at Otto, one of Mario Batali's joints in New York City, and we were inspired by that. This ice cream recipe is one of the simplest in the book, and that's because we definitely want you to try it. Olive oil ain't just for dunking your bread in, people!

1 cup heavy cream

¾ cup whole milk

½ cup sugar

¼ cup extra-virgin olive oil

½ cup Fig Sauce (optional; page 63)

A few pinches of coarse sea salt or fleur de sel

Warm the cream and milk in a medium saucepan over medium heat, stirring often, for about 5 minutes, until the mixture begins to steam. Add the sugar and stir for about 3 minutes, until completely dissolved. Slowly add the olive oil, whisking continuously, then continue to cook for another 5 minutes, whisking frequently.

Remove from the heat and transfer the mixture to a 1-quart container. Cover and refrigerate for at least 6 hours.

Thoroughly whisk the chilled mixture until fully reincorporated (the oil will have separated slightly overnight) and freeze in an ice cream maker according to the manufacturer's instructions. If using, slowly pour in the fig sauce during the machine's mix-in phase. When it is finished, enjoy right away or transfer the ice cream to an airtight container and freeze for up to 4 hours to harden.

Right before serving, sprinkle a few pinches of sea salt onto the ice cream.

Sweet Cream Ice Cream (Custard) MAKES 1 QUART

Ice creams made with eggs take a bit more time and patience because you have to cook a custard base, without turning it into scrambled eggs. These ice creams hold up better in your freezer than Philly-style because the egg yolks act as an emulsifier, keeping iciness at bay. Additionally, they will stay semisoft over a longer period of time, retaining that luscious creaminess you think of when you think of fresh homemade ice cream.

5 large egg yolks

1½ cups whole milk

1½ cups heavy cream

⅔ cup sugar

½ teaspoon coarse sea salt

Whisk the egg yolks in a large nonreactive saucepan; set aside. Warm the milk and cream in a small saucepan over medium heat, stirring often to keep the mixture from scorching for about 5 minutes, until it has begun to steam. Add the mixture to the yolks in a slow, steady stream, whisking continuously.

Set the saucepan over medium heat, add the sugar and salt, and stir for about 2 minutes, until the sugar has dissolved. Continue cooking, stirring continuously, for another 5 minutes, or until the mixture begins to thicken; do not allow to boil. Transfer the pan to an ice bath to stop the cooking and stir until the steaming stops.

Transfer the mixture to an airtight container, cover, and refrigerate for at least 6 hours, or preferably overnight.

Freeze the mixture in an ice cream maker according to the manufacturer's instructions. When it is finished, transfer the ice cream to an airtight container and freeze for at least 2 hours to harden. The ice cream can be stored in the freezer for up to 5 days.

Vanilla Ice Cream

MAKES 1 QUART

Oh, vanilla ice cream. You're a tough one, because so many people are used to tasting way too much vanilla in you! With awesome dairy and sugar as the backbone of your homemade ice cream, you'll want only a slight touch of vanilla. For this recipe, we use high-quality vanilla extract (such as Nielsen-Massey) because it's both cheaper and quicker than using vanilla beans. Try swapping in different brands for subsequent batches, or mix and match and blend your own custom extract. It's okay with us if you never make this recipe the same way twice.

5 large egg yolks

1½ cups whole milk

1½ cups heavy cream

2 teaspoons pure vanilla extract (no fake stuff!)

⅔ cup sugar

½ teaspoon coarse sea salt

Whisk the egg yolks in a large nonreactive saucepan; set aside. Warm the milk and cream in a small saucepan over medium heat, stirring often to keep the mixture from scorching, for about 5 minutes, until it has begun to steam. Add the mixture to the yolks in a slow, steady stream, whisking continuously.

Set the saucepan over medium heat, add the vanilla, sugar, and salt, and stir for about 2 minutes, until the sugar has dissolved. Continue cooking, stirring continuously, for another 5 minutes, or until the mixture begins to thicken; do not allow to boil. Transfer the pan to an ice bath to stop the cooking and stir until the steaming stops.

Transfer the mixture to an airtight container, cover, and refrigerate for at least 6 hours, or overnight.

Freeze the mixture in an ice cream maker according to the manufacturer's instructions. When it is finished, transfer the ice cream to an airtight container and freeze for at least 2 hours to harden. The ice cream can be stored in the freezer for up to 5 days.

Milk Chocolate Ice Cream MAKES 1 QUART

You can never have enough chocolate, so we've also included an egg-based chocolate ice cream recipe for you. This recipe uses milk chocolate, making it a bit lighter than the eggless version. Don't get us wrong: It still tastes great on its own, but it's also flavored lightly enough to pair well with any toppings you want to throw at (or in) it.

You can eat this straight out of the ice cream machine with a fruit spread dolloped atop or as an ice cream base for any chunky, crunchy, sweet, or salty mix-in, such as in our Rocky Road House Ice Cream (page 172). Milk it for all it's worth!

5 large egg yolks

1½ cups whole milk

1½ cups heavy cream

2 tablespoons unsweetened cocoa powder

½ teaspoon kosher salt

1 teaspoon pure vanilla extract

⅓ cup sugar

6 ounces milk chocolate morsels or finely chopped milk chocolate bar

Whisk the egg yolks in a large nonreactive saucepan; set aside. Warm the milk and cream in a small saucepan over medium heat, stirring often to keep the mixture from scorching, for about 5 minutes, until it has begun to steam. Whisk in the cocoa powder and salt until dissolved. Add the mixture to the yolks in a slow, steady stream, whisking continuously.

Set the saucepan over medium heat, add the vanilla and sugar, and stir for about 2 minutes, until the sugar has dissolved. Continue cooking, stirring continuously, for another 5 minutes, or until the mixture begins to thicken; do not allow to boil. Remove from the heat and whisk in the milk chocolate for no more than 45 seconds, to thoroughly incorporate. Transfer the pan to an ice bath to stop the cooking and stir until the steaming stops.

Transfer the mixture to an airtight container, cover, and refrigerate for at least 6 hours.

The chilled mixture will be quite thick, so give it a good whisk before pouring it into your ice cream maker. Freeze according to the manufacturer's instructions. When it is finished, transfer the ice cream to an airtight container and freeze for at least 2 hours to harden. The ice cream can be stored in the freezer for up to 5 days.

SCIENCE CLUB

What Is an Emulsifier? Why Do I Need One to Make Ice Cream?

We all know that oil and water don't mix. That's because oil is *hydrophobic,* which is a fancy word meaning that it doesn't like water. So it tends to hang out in its own little clique, as separate as possible from any water. Think about salad dressing—the oil and vinegar usually separate into two very distinct layers. You can shake the container of dressing hard (or whisk it) and break up the oil into lots and lots of smaller droplets which will be suspended in the vinegar. But if you let it sit, eventually the oil separates out again so that you have two distinct layers. If you look at the variety of salad dressings at the grocery store, you may see some vinaigrettes that don't look like two layers. Check the ingredient list—you will find an emulsifier. With ice cream, the ice plays the part of the water and the cream plays the part of the oil. You wouldn't want ice cream that is separated into ice and cream, you want everybody to get along. An emulsifier plays the role of peacekeeper. It's made up of molecules that have one end that likes fat and one end that likes water. It holds these two together, so everything stays well mixed and doesn't separate. Some common emulsifiers are egg yolks, some dairy products, seaweed extracts (such as carrageenan), lecithin, xanthan gum, cellulose gum, and various types of glycerides.

This kumbaya moment stays around after the ice cream base is frozen, allowing the ice cream ingredients to stay solid enough to bind together, but not so strongly that they become an ice cream brick.

Cardamom Ice Cream

MAKES 1 QUART

Cardamom is a unique ingredient. Many people ask us what it is, thinking they aren't familiar with it, but we give them a pinch to smell, and they instantly recognize it from Indian cooking. More than simply flavoring a food, it gives it a fragrance. With both cardamom and vanilla, this ice cream fills your mouth with flavor in the way few other combinations can. We think it's pretty goddamned interesting and even more goddamned delicious.

5 large egg yolks

2 cups heavy cream

1½ cups whole milk

2 tablespoons ground cardamom

A small handful of cardamom pods (about 10), crushed with the side of a chef's knife

1 teaspoon pure vanilla extract

¾ cup sugar

½ teaspoon coarse sea salt

Whisk the egg yolks in a large nonreactive saucepan; set aside. Warm the cream, milk, ground cardamom, and crushed cardamom pods in a medium saucepan over medium-low heat, stirring often to keep the mixture from scorching, for 15 minutes, until very aromatic. Add the mixture (it's fine to leave the pods in for this step—you'll strain them out later) to the yolks in a slow, steady stream, whisking continuously.

Set the saucepan over medium-low heat, add the vanilla, sugar, and salt, and stir for about 2 minutes, until the sugar has dissolved. Continue cooking, stirring continuously, for another 5 minutes, or until the mixture begins to thicken; do not allow to boil. Transfer the pan to an ice bath to stop the cooking and stir until the steaming stops.

Pour the mixture through a sieve to remove the cardamom pods and seeds, transfer to an airtight container, cover, and refrigerate for at least 6 hours.

Freeze the mixture in an ice cream maker according to the manufacturer's instructions. When it is finished, transfer the ice cream to an airtight container and freeze for at least 2 hours to harden. The ice cream can be stored in the freezer for up to 5 days.

Dirty Banana
Ice Cream MAKES 1 QUART

Bananas, butter, and brown sugar. What else do you need? Some eggs and cream will help, but there's no need to look much further. Let those bananas really carmelize. With just a little bit of butter and sugar, and a quick dip in a sauté pan, everything is so much better.

1 ripe medium to large banana (with brown spots on the skin)

4 tablespoons unsalted butter

⅔ cup lightly packed dark brown sugar

5 large egg yolks

2 cups whole milk

1¼ cups heavy cream

1½ teaspoons pure vanilla extract

½ teaspoon kosher salt

Slice the banana into ½-inch-thick circles. Melt the butter in a small sauté pan over medium-high heat. The butter needs to be quite hot (but not burning) for the bananas to properly caramelize; otherwise, the bananas will just absorb the butter and turn mushy. Place the banana slices in the pan and sauté until the first side has browned, then flip. Once the bananas are nicely browned on the second side, sprinkle the brown sugar over them and allow it to melt. Stir the bananas and sugar to combine and set aside.

Whisk the egg yolks in a large nonreactive saucepan; set aside. Warm the milk and cream in a medium saucepan over medium heat, stirring often to keep the mixture from scorching, for about 5 minutes, until it has begun to steam. Add the mixture to the yolks in a slow, steady stream, whisking continuously.

Set the saucepan over medium heat, add the vanilla and salt, and stir to combine. Add the banana mixture, then whisk together, mashing the bananas thoroughly. Cook, stirring continuously, for 7 to 10 minutes, until the mixture begins to thicken; do not allow to boil. Transfer the pan to an ice bath to stop the cooking and stir until the steaming stops. Transfer the mixture to an airtight container, cover, and refrigerate for at least 6 hours.

Freeze the mixture in an ice cream maker according to the manufacturer's instructions. When it is finished, transfer the ice cream to an airtight container and freeze for at least 2 hours to harden. Store in the freezer for up to 5 days.

Big Gay Ice Cream
Yes Please
Extra cream Please

Coconut Ice Cream

MAKES 1 QUART

The best thing about the television show *Gilligan's Island* was probably that it made us all so curious about coconuts. If the castaways weren't using them as clothing, or to repair radios, or to buttress their huts, they were making countless coconut pies. What the hell did Mary Ann make the crust with? Did they bake their coconut pies in ovens made of coconuts and powered by coconut oil? Why didn't Gilligan learn that a nap under a coconut tree meant an inevitable concussion and then paranoid dreams or amnesia? If coconuts are capable of supertechnologies, couldn't they have left the island aboard a teleportation device powered by coco-dilithium crystals magnified with a coconut flux capacitor? Shh! Too many questions! Make this simple coconut ice cream, which uses creamed coconut. If you can't find creamed coconut locally, definitely order some online—it's worth tracking down.

4 large egg yolks

1½ cups whole milk

¾ cup heavy cream

1 cup sugar

One 7-ounce package creamed coconut

½ teaspoon coconut extract

½ teaspoon kosher salt

Whisk the egg yolks in a large nonreactive saucepan; set aside. Warm the milk and cream in a small saucepan over medium heat, stirring often to keep the mixture from scorching, for about 5 minutes, until it has begun to steam. Add the mixture to the yolks in a slow, steady stream, whisking continuously.

Set the saucepan over medium heat, add the sugar, and stir for about 2 minutes, until the sugar has dissolved. Add the creamed coconut, coconut extract, and salt and stir to thoroughly incorporate. Continue cooking, stirring continuously, for another 8 minutes, or until the mixture begins to thicken; do not allow to boil. Transfer the pan to an ice bath to stop the cooking and stir until the steaming stops.

Transfer the mixture to an airtight container, cover, and refrigerate for at least 6 hours.

Freeze the mixture in an ice cream maker according to the manufacturer's instructions. When it is finished, transfer the ice cream to an airtight container and freeze for at least 2 hours to harden. Store in the freezer for up to 5 days.

Peppermint Ice Cream

MAKES 1 QUART

Oh, peppermint. We first loved you because of Peppermint Patty in *Peanuts,* with whom we strangely identified as kids (geez, no idea why). Peppermint tastes so damned great when done right, but when someone just dumps cheap peppermint-*flavored* syrup into a product? Yuck. A little peppermint extract is good to punch up the flavoring, but if you really want peppermint flavor to work, YOU need to work. There's going to be some shopping, chopping, steeping, and colandering (not a word, just let us have this) involved, but the payoff is so worth it!

4 large egg yolks

1½ cups whole milk

1½ cups heavy cream

1 cup loosely packed fresh mint leaves, coarsely chopped

½ cup loosely packed fresh basil leaves, coarsely chopped

2 heaping tablespoons whole black peppercorns

1 teaspoon peppermint extract

⅔ cup sugar

Whisk the egg yolks in a large nonreactive saucepan; set aside. Warm the milk, cream, mint, basil, and peppercorns in a medium saucepan over medium-low heat for 20 minutes, stirring often to keep the mixture from scorching.

Pour the mixture through a strainer into a medium bowl to remove all the solids, pressing down with a whisk or ricer to release as much of the liquid as possible; discard the solids. Add the mixture to the yolks in a slow, steady stream, whisking continuously. Set the saucepan over medium heat, add the peppermint extract and sugar, and stir for about 2 minutes, until the sugar has dissolved. Continue cooking, stirring continuously, for another 5 minutes, or until the mixture begins to thicken; do not allow to boil. Transfer the pan to an ice bath to stop the cooking and stir until the steaming stops.

Transfer the mixture to an airtight container, cover, and refrigerate for at least 6 hours.

Freeze the mixture in an ice cream maker according to the manufacturer's instructions. When it is finished, transfer the ice cream to an airtight container and freeze for at least 2 hours to harden. The ice cream can be stored in the freezer for up to 5 days.

Love you guys!
Big Gay everyday
Rocco ☆ FAHRENHEIT

Pumpkin Ice Cream

MAKES 1 QUART

Pumpkin soft-serve is one of our frequent special offerings at our shops. Coming up with the recipe was a bit of a challenge, because at first it ended up tasting a bit too much like either straight-up pumpkin pie (not so bad) or potpourri (not so good). It turned out that the pumpkin pie spice combination wasn't that far off, just way too strong. We dialed things back, allowing the pumpkin flavor to step to the forefront. Right where it should be.

5 large egg yolks

1¾ cups heavy cream

¾ cup whole milk

½ teaspoon ground allspice

½ teaspoon ground cloves

½ teaspoon ground cinnamon

¼ teaspoon cayenne pepper

½ teaspoon ground nutmeg

¾ teaspoon kosher salt

¾ cup lightly packed dark brown sugar

¾ teaspoon pure vanilla extract

2 tablespoons maple syrup

1 cup canned pumpkin puree (not pumpkin pie mix)

Whisk the egg yolks in a large nonreactive saucepan; set aside. Warm the cream and milk in a small saucepan over medium heat, stirring often to keep the mixture from scorching, for about 5 minutes, until it has begun to steam. Add the mixture to the yolks in a slow, steady stream, whisking continuously.

Set the saucepan over medium heat, add the allspice, cloves, cinnamon, cayenne, nutmeg, salt, and brown sugar and stir until the sugar has dissolved. Add the vanilla and maple syrup and stir to combine. Add the canned pumpkin and cook, stirring continuously, for 10 minutes, or until the mixture starts to thicken; do not allow to boil. Transfer the pan to an ice bath to stop the cooking and stir until the steaming stops.

Transfer the mixture to an airtight container, cover, and refrigerate for at least 6 hours.

Freeze the mixture in an ice cream maker according to the manufacturer's instructions. When it is finished, transfer the ice cream to an airtight container and freeze for at least 2 hours to harden. The ice cream can be stored in the freezer for up to 5 days.

Bea Arthur Ice Cream (Chunky-Style)

MAKES ABOUT 5 CUPS

Beloved Ms. Arthur: as you gaze down upon us from that lanai in the sky with a stiff drink in your hand, we ask that you please forgive us for using your name and the descriptive term "chunky" in the same recipe. By no means are we making a reference to your figure. It's just that this ice cream flavor is based on your soft-serve namesake, and it's, well, chunky.

Also, please don't take it personally when Doug finally gets around to commissioning that mural he wants with your head on a minotaur's body. Thanks in advance, Bryan (& Doug).

½ cup Nilla wafer cookies, broken up into small pieces

¼ cup Dulce de Leche (page 57)

1 quart Vanilla Ice Cream (page 157)

Place the Nilla wafer pieces in the freezer for 1 hour. Place a 9-inch round cake pan or large bowl in the freezer to chill.

Smear the dulce de leche over the bottom of the cake pan. Add the ice cream to the pan, then add the cookies and use a spatula to gently fold all the ingredients together, working fast so the ice cream doesn't melt. Transfer the ice cream to an airtight container and freeze for at least 6 hours, or overnight, to harden. The ice cream can be stored in the freezer for up to 5 days.

IN BEA WE TRUST

Rocky Road House Ice Cream
MAKES 1 QUART

Patrick Swayze made a few of the most important movies out there. *Red Dawn; Skatetown, U.S.A.;* and *Point Break* are all masterpieces, but none of them approach his greatest opus, and our favorite, in the Swayzeography—*Road House*. Such a great man clearly deserves every tribute that comes his way. Doug declared that Swayzepalooza would be celebrated every August 18 (Mr. Swayze's birthday) at our shops, and thus Rocky Road House was born.

Our version of this classic flavor uses the traditional mix-ins, but makes them a little extra gooey and therefore a little extra delicious. The ice cream base is milk chocolate—it's very rich, but allows the dark chocolate mix-in to really stand out.

½ cup slivered almonds

1 cup miniature marshmallows

½ cup dark chocolate (morsels or coarsely chopped)

Generous dash of coarse sea salt

Base for Milk Chocolate Ice Cream (page 158), thoroughly chilled

Preheat the oven to 350°F. Spread the almonds on a baking sheet and toast until golden brown, about 5 minutes (do not burn). Transfer to a medium bowl and add the marshmallows and dark chocolate, stirring to combine, until the chocolate begins to melt. Stir in the salt. Cover the bowl with plastic wrap or an airtight lid and place in the freezer to chill completely.

Freeze the milk chocolate base in an ice cream maker according to the manufacturer's instructions.

Meanwhile, place a large mixing bowl in the freezer to chill.

Remove the almond mixture from the freezer and, using your hands or a fork, break it up into bite-size pieces. When the ice cream is finished, transfer it to the chilled mixing bowl and use a spatula to quickly fold in the broken-up almond mixture. Begin eating or transfer to an airtight container and freeze for at least 6 hours to harden. The ice cream can be stored in the freezer for up to 5 days.

NOTE: Because the mix-ins are too big for most ice cream machines to accommodate, fold them in using a spatula and a chilled bowl.

Tangerine-Mezcal Ice Cream

MAKES 1 QUART

Fany Gerson is the one person on this earth who makes us wish we were fabulously wealthy Saudi royalty. Once we finally ARE fabulously wealthy Saudi royalty, we will give Fany free rein as our palace chef so we can eat her amazing food every day and she can regale us with her weird stories about stalker nannies when she was growing up in Mexico. Fany can cook anything (including Thanksgiving dinner for thirty-five people in a small Manhattan studio apartment), but the world may know her best for her *paletas* (Mexican fruit pops) and her sweets (both sold under her La Newyorkina moniker). Her ice cream flavors marry so well with ours that we just had to include one. Make this. When you taste it, you'll understand why it's impossible not to love Fany. *Jajajaja!*

1½ cups heavy cream

1 cup whole milk

1 vanilla bean, split lengthwise, seeds scraped out and reserved

¾ cup plus 2 tablespoons sugar

4 teaspoons finely grated tangerine zest

¼ teaspoon salt

6 large egg yolks

⅔ cup fresh tangerine juice

⅓ cup mezcal

NOTE: If tangerines and mezcal are hard to find, substitute oranges and tequila.

Combine the cream, milk, vanilla seeds, sugar, zest, and salt in a medium heavy saucepan and bring to a boil over medium heat, stirring often. Remove from the heat.

Whisk the egg yolks in a medium bowl until blended. Add about half of the hot cream mixture in a slow, steady stream, whisking continuously. Transfer the egg-cream mixture to the saucepan and cook over medium-low heat, stirring constantly, until the mixture is thick enough to coat the back of a spoon; do not allow to boil.

Immediately strain through a fine-mesh sieve into a medium bowl, then stir in the tangerine juice. Let cool to room temperature, stirring occasionally.

Add the mezcal to the mixture. Transfer to an airtight container, cover, and chill in the refrigerator for at least 6 hours.

Freeze the mixture in an ice cream maker according to the manufacturer's instructions. When it is finished, transfer the ice cream to an airtight container and freeze for at least 4 hours to harden. The ice cream can be stored in the freezer for up to 5 days.

Ice Cream Social Playlist

60 UR

POSITION
IEC TYPE I • NORMAL

CHRISTMAS ON THE
FOURTH OF JULY

A

AC/DC
"It's a Long Way
to the Top"

The Runaways
"Cherry Bomb"

Deee-Lite
"Power of Love"

Tom Petty & The Heartbreakers
"American Girl"

The Jim Carroll Band
"People Who Died"

Daft Punk
"Get Lucky"

Led Zeppelin
"D'yer Mak'er"

Major Lazer
"Bubble Butt"

Cornershop
"Brimful of Asha"

B

Ike & Tina Turner
"Nutbush City Limits"

Ozzy Osborne
"Crazy Train"

Fire Inc
"Nowhere Fast"

Berlin
"The Metro"

Quiet Riot
"Cum On Feel the Noize"

Michael Jackson
"Wanna Be Startin'
Somethin'"

DJ Cutlet
"Big Gay Ice Cream Truck"

Jane Wiedlin
"Big Gay Ice Cream Song"

U.S.A.

Pow

BOOM!

NORTH POLE

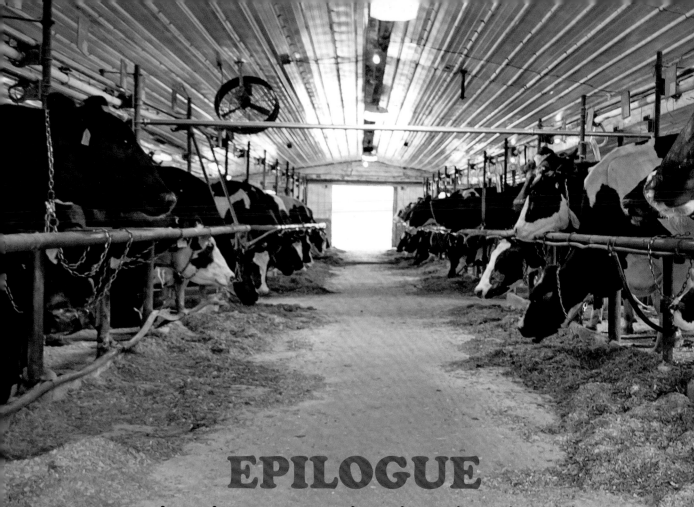

EPILOGUE

Senior Trip—to Ronnybrook and Back Again

The Cosmos and Gail Simmons

We never decided to have a business together—it just happened. And now we refer to it as the little summer project that consumed our lives. Or possibly it's a midlife crisis, but one involving beat-up ice cream trucks instead of flashy convertibles. The effervescent Gail Simmons had a much more elegant (and cosmic) way of saying it. While helping us serve hundreds of Mermaid Sundaes to an endless queue of people on the white sands of South Beach, she told us, "Big Gay Ice Cream has always existed, out there in the universe. It was traveling through space like a comet, waiting

for just the right moment to land on earth, and it found that in you two." Pardon us while we reach for our hankies. We ♥ Gail.

So what did it see in us, two bald and gray guys *approaching* middle age? Well, we are certainly still kids at heart, and as we said in the beginning, there's no food more fun than ice cream. We are lucky to do what we love and have a ball doing it. Youth, so we say, is wasted on the young.

Writing and publishing, especially when it comes to cookbooks, takes a long time. Case in point: this little epilogue was written a full

year after the entire manuscript. An awful lot has happened to our Big Gay world in that year, which we are fortunate to be able to mention now. When we started the book, we were a not-so-big business based in New York City. Now we are certainly bigger, if not gayer, with additional stores in Los Angeles and Philadelphia. Big Gay has gone national, with more on the way.

Year after year this roller-coaster ride gets wilder and crazier. Scary? Sure. But worth all the E-tickets you can find. This growth couldn't have happened, however, without first taking care of a few critical factors behind the scenes.

A Few Critical Factors Behind the Scenes

Part of what has gotten the two of us over the hurdle from trembling freshmen to lofty seniors is our love of learning new things and our continuing ambition to be better at what we do, year after year.

The biggest challenge we gave ourselves over the last year or so was shifting to have as many of our dishes as possible be homemade and based on our own recipes. As we get bigger, we are actually producing more in-house—the opposite of most growing companies. Take, for example, our Dulce de Leche (page 57). We use the same recipe for DDL in our shops that we have here in our book—it costs us three times as much to make compared with the price of commercial versions, and we ultimately decided to eat the cost ourselves instead of raising our prices. As a matter of fact, there has been a lot of crossover between what's in this book and

what's in our shops. It's that kind of attention to service and quality that we hope you both see and taste.

But even before we tackled sauces and toppings, we tackled the ice cream itself. Undoubtedly the biggest decision we made (snugly in our junior year) was to leave the world of commercial ice cream and mixes and make our own ice cream from scratch. We knew we were not in a position to make it ourselves in our teeny tiny shops. So we threw caution to the wind and went right to the best dairy we could find: Ronnybrook Farm Dairy, in Ancramdale, New York, and their resident ice cream scientist, John LeSauvage (an ice cream Gandalf if there ever was one). The result was our own secret recipe—a proprietary ice cream manufactured right at the farm (and different from Ronnybrook's house-label ice cream) and delivered to our shops ready to freeze. We still get the satisfaction of being creative in the shops with bases that we can doctor up into all sorts of daily and weekly special flavors. Working with Ronnybrook this way enables us to continue to grow as a brand without compromising or re-envisioning our business model.

Introducing Ronnybrook

We know a lot of people may question the state (and fate) of domesticated animals in the United States, but certainly the last place to take your picket sign and megaphone is Ronnybrook Farm Dairy.

Our business is the first commercial partnership Ronnybrook has ever made (at least in recent memory). They've been approached by a number of "artisan" ice cream companies over the years, and have always said no to making a base for them. We are still trying to figure out what they saw in us, but it may just be as simple as finding kindred spirits.

So what's there to know about Ronnybrook? Well, as we found out through our trips to the farm, both individually and with our employees, lots actually.

Ronnybrook is a small family-run farm in the Hudson Valley near the Catskills, a few hours north of New York City, with a herd of 300 to 400 cows. They raise and milk their own cows, manufacture their own line of dairy products, and deliver them in their own trucks. We (not so jokingly) say that if you time it right, the ice cream in your Pimp or Bea has gone from the cow's teat to your tongue in about three days. It's homemade ice cream the way it should be— freshly made and rarely frozen (well, until it is run through our machines at the shops).

The cows' primary diet is the pasture they graze on, supplemented by hay and feed grown on the farm. No growth hormones, chemicals, or additives are in their milk. The cows are allowed to come and go as they please, hang in the barn or out in the sun on the 1,000 acres of the farm, and they get to sleep on "cow-tresses," individual mattresses for every cow. Having only a few hundred cows on that much land means lots of room for them to roam. The last time we were there, we caught one of them (we think her name was Lily) curled up under a tree on the far side of a hill tearing through the latest Nicholas Sparks novel.

Ronnybrook has been called "beyond organic" by the *New York Times*, but their milk is not Certified Organic. Why? The biggest reason is they treat their cows with medication when they are sick. This is a no-no in the organic community, which would rather send a cow "out to pasture" than nurse it back to health. Ronnybrook believes their cows are part of their family. They care for them as we would our pets, medicating them when they're sick and keeping newborns protected until they're old enough to care for themselves. Because, let's face it: while cows may have long pretty eyelashes and distinct personalities, they aren't the brightest animals on the farm. But treating them when they're sick doesn't mean that there are antibiotics in their milk. Sick cows are segregated and cared for until they're healthy enough to return to the herd. All of the milk on the farm is tested daily, and only milk that tests 100 percent pure makes it to your refrigerator. The practices employed at Ronnybrook—doing everything themselves, the ratio of cow to acre of land, and their special brand of bovine care and raising—actually cost more than the requirements to be Certified Organic. But they believe—as we do—that it is worth it for both the animals and the milk they produce.

They are also a bit odd (as all farmers are), but they're the nicest people on the planet, make a mean BBQ spread for guests, and put up with weird city folk types who want to take silly "class trip" photos for their cookbooks.

Excelsior!

It's our relationship with Ronnybrook that we use as our model for store growth.

When we decided to open in California, the first thing we told ourselves was, "There's no way in hell we are going to ship frozen mix across the country." What's the point of focusing so much energy on quality of product and local farms and markets if you turn around and explode your carbon footprint by shipping it three thousand miles away? News flash: There are wonderful dairies all over this country (and in Canada), as well as myriad sources for great fruits and nuts and everything else we use.

The focus of our store growth has a lot to do with building relationships with those dairies and farmers. Our stores in both the New York and Los Angeles markets each use dairy from cows that live only two hours away: at Ronnybrook in the verdant hills of the Hudson Valley and in the sunshine of the San Jacinto Valley near Palm Springs on the West Coast.

So where do we go from here? What's in our Big Gay future? We aren't too sure ourselves, to be honest, but we aren't worried about discovering it. It will find us. Only the cosmos knows for sure. And Gail Simmons.

ACKNOWLEDGMENTS

Everything that has come our way in the last few years has been totally unexpected. It's been a wild ride, and we continue to be surprised and excited at each turn—as much as we were during that first summer. We still sit back and stare at each other in bemused bewilderment, then burst out into laughter. We take nothing for granted and we love every minute of it—even the parts that can seem completely overwhelming and unsurmountable. Thankfully, the time when it will stop being fun and surprising feels nowhere in sight.

All of it—the truck, the stores, the love, the customers, the unexpected friendships, our recipes, even the ninety-minute waits for a Salty ("procurer"), and, of course, this book—has been beyond our wildest dreams. And as we continue to envision and plan for our Big Gay Future, we can't wait to see what comes next, and we hope you'll continue to join us for the ride.

Cool Kids

This book was no small undertaking. In fact, it took almost three and a half years from our very first meeting with the folks from Clarkson Potter to the time this finished product hit bookshelves. During that time, the following people contributed everything from time and energy to valuable feedback and inspiration to a shoulder to cry on. We couldn't have done it without all of you:

Everyone who helped make this book happen: Pam Krauss, Emily Takoudes, Jane Treuhaft,

Judith Sutton, Aaron Wehner, Doris Cooper, and Jessica Freeman-Slade at Clarkson Potter; Cait Hoyt, Simon Green, and Lisa Shotland at CAA; Phil Colicchio, lawyer extraordinaire; and our great friends and contributors Rebecca Flint Marx, Donny Tsang, Michael Condran, Anthony Bourdain, Sarah Thyre, Michael Kupperman, Kim Brisack, Bill Morrison, and Jason O'Malley.

Our recipe contributors: Fany Gerson, Jake Godby, John T. Edge, Ann Grosz, Kim Ima, and Jenn Louis.

Our writing contributors: Neil Gaiman, Stacy London, Gail Simmons, Andrew Zimmern, Jon Shook, Vinny Dotolo, Andrea Fisher, Rachael Ray, Kim Severson, Dana Delany, and Valerie Frankel.

Our recipe testers: Rebecca Masson, Tommy Lee, Ninja Kimberly, Katzie Guy-Hamilton, Jim Ginter, and Will Richter.

Our ultrafabulous and invaluable employees, who held down the forts when we cloistered ourselves to write the book and develop the recipes. Glenna, Gary, and Kayla: you guys. YOU GUYS!

Our friends, who have kept us sane and levelheaded when we were at our craziest and convinced the sky was falling: Ottavia Bourdain, Ariane Bourdain, J. Eric Small, Karen Isaacs, Jodi Lennon, Andy Richter, Mercy Richter, Darin

Bresnitz, Greg Bresnitz, Mary Smith, Mary Alice Fallon Yeskey, Debi Mazar, Gina Schock, Kat Kinsman, Erin Orlovsky-Oldershaw, Pete Contreri, Genevieve Belleveau, Benjamin Turley, Emma Griffiths, Helen Johannesen, Richard Sawka II, Felicia Pugh, Gordon Robinson, JR Craigmile, Rishia Zimmern, Dusti Kugler, Molly Mogren, Sarah De Sa Rego, and William E. Taft. Chapski, you get thanked too.

Our customers, who keep this crazy wheel spinning—especially all the original regulars back at 17th Street and Broadway. You insisted that we succeed.

The Morelli and Holland families: you fueled up the truck because you believe in magic.

Our chef and restaurant-owner friends who are much more talented than we will ever be: David McMillan, Fred Morin, Vanya Filipovic, and Marc-Olivier Frappier; Marc Vetri, Jeff Benjamin, Brad Spence, Adam Leonti, Jeff Michaud, Brad Daniels, and Ned Maddock; Andy Ricker; Marco Canora and George Kaden; Ludo Lefebvre; Martin Picard; Kevin Sbraga; Anne Burrell; Carla Hall; Zac Young; Ricky Webster; Spike Mendelsohn; Johnny Iuzzini; and Sarah Simmons.

Our ice cream connections: David Lebovitz; Gus and Mimi Rancantore; Sean Greenwood; Julian Plyter and Kareem Hamady; Katy Peetz; Meredith Kurtzman; the team at Little Baby's Ice Cream; and a special salute to John Lesauvage and to Rick and Ronny at Ronnybrook.

Our muses: Michael Caterisano (aka DJ Cutlet) and the multitalented and highly complex Jane Marie Genevieve Wiedlin.

WHERE TO SHOP

If you want to branch out beyond your local store, here are some of our favorite places for inspiration and ingredients.

Appetite for Books
cookbook store with a demo kitchen for visiting chefs

AppetiteBooks.ca
388 av. Victoria
Montreal, QC J4P 2H8 Canada

Auberge J. A. Moisan
the oldest grocery store in North America, this spot has an amazing array of items that are perfect company for ice cream

JAMoisan.com
695 rue Saint-Jean
Québec, QC G1R 1P7 Canada

Bierkraft
international foods, an amazing beer collection, and their own prepared foods

Bierkraft.com
191 5th Avenue
Brooklyn, NY 11215

Economy Candy
four walls and a roof packed with so much candy they have a dentist's office in the back—well, not really; they also have nuts and dried fruits

EconomyCandy.com
108 Rivington Street
New York, NY 10002

Fairway
New York City's premier supermarket

Fairway.com
multiple locations

Kalustyan's
international foods and spices

Kalustyans.com
123 Lexington Avenue
New York, NY 10016

The Meat Hook
you know you love bacon, so get the best bacon you can from this butcher shop

The-MeatHook.com
100 Frost Street
Brooklyn, NY 11211

Murray's Cheese Shop
New York's iconic cheese shop also has a huge array of specialty foods and ingredients

MurraysCheese.com
multiple locations

Olives & Épices
quite possibly the best single source for spices and oils from around the world

OliveOlives.com
7070 Henri-Julien Avenue
Jean-Talon Market
Montreal, QC H2R 1T1 Canada

Quin Candy and Shane Confectionery
if you insist on topping ice cream with candy, use the best

QuinCandy.com
1025 SW Stark Street
Portland, OR 97205

ShaneCandies.com
110 Market Street
Philadelphia, PA 19106

Stonewall Kitchen
high-quality prepared foods, both sweet and savory

StonewallKitchen.com
multiple locations

The Treats Truck Stop
all your baked-good needs for any ice cream social

TreatsTruck.com
521 Court Street
Brooklyn, NY 11231

Whole Foods
a great selection of high-quality and unique or hard-to-find ingredients, as well as dietary-specific foods

WholeFoods.com
multiple locations

World Spice Merchants
spices, blends, teas, coffees, and more

WorldSpice.com
1509 Western Avenue
Seattle, WA 98101

Local farmers' markets are great resources for fruit, sweet veggies (fennel, carrots), honeys, syrups, vinegars, jams, nuts, fruit butters, and more. While there are countless great markets all over the United States and Canada, we swoon every time we go to the **Marin Farmers' Market** in San Rafael and the **Santa Monica Farmers' Markets** in California, and the **Jean-Talon** and **Atwater Markets** in Montreal.

Local bakeries are, obviously, a great source for cookies and other pastry items. In addition to The Treats Truck Stop (see above) we love **Baked** (BakedNYC.com) in Brooklyn, **Fluff Bake Bar** (FluffBakeBar.com) in Houston, and **Scratch Baking Co.** (ScratchBakingCo.com) in South Portland, Maine.

A FEW OF OUR FAVORITE THINGS

Cacao Nibs
Taza Chocolate
TazaChocolate.com

Cocoa Powder
Valrhona
Valrhona-Chocolate.com

Coconut
Let's Do . . . Organic (yep, that's the brand name)
EdwardAndSons.com

Coffee
Big Gay Blend (of course!)
available in our shops or online at
BigGayIceCream.com

Fruit Butters
McCutcheon's
BobMcCutcheon.com

Ginger Syrup
The Ginger People
GingerPeople.com

Maple Syrup
Coombs Family Farms Grade B
CoombsFamilyFarms.com

Mezcal
Fidencio de Pechuga
FidencioMezcal.com

Olive Oil
Bariani (California) and La Belle Excuse (Quebec)
Bariani.com
LaBelleExcuse.com

Peanut Butter
Skippy (smooth) and Smucker's Natural (chunky)
PeanutButter.com (Skippy)
Smuckers.com

Pistachios
Heart of the Desert
HeartOfTheDesert.com

Pretzels
Unique Extra Dark Splits
UniqueSplits.com

Teas
Harney & Sons
Harney.com

Tequila
Chinaco
ChinacoTequila.com

Wet Wipes (because things get messy)
Herban Essentials
HerbanEssentials.com

There are a number of items mentioned in this book that may be hard to find, such as saba, lemongrass, and elderflower liqueur. Honestly, your best bet for finding them is online. Start with the mother of all online stores, **Amazon.com.**

BIG KISSES!
BOOBALICOUS!
CHARLIE BOYS

Index